Take One Garden ...

Flavours from
Dr Neil's Garden, Duddingston

Susan Mercer

Silver Spade Books
Jumped Up Publishing Ltd

Published by Silver Spade Books in 2006

From Jumped Up Publishing Ltd
107 Joppa Road
Edinburgh EH15 2HB
Email: jumpedupbooks@yahoo.com

ISBN: 978-0955364-1-05
0-9553641-0-8

INTRODUCTION

Dr Neil's Garden is a surprising place. Sometimes called the Secret Garden, it is tucked between Duddingston Kirk and the Loch, so that you need directions in order to find it. Once there, you can see that the sharply sloping site, together with the tree and shrub cover, mean that it is impossible to view the whole of the garden from any one point. The bedrock is a visible feature in several places, and, indeed, the rock is nowhere far below the surface. The garden has been constructed, therefore, as a series of stepped terraces, so that there are many miniature gardens-within-a-garden. The horizon to the northwest is filled with the bulk of Arthur's Seat; the tower and roof of the Kirk form the view to the north; and looking south, on the far horizon are the Pentland Hills, but immediately, from east to west, lies the body of water which is Duddingston Loch. In the garden you are constantly aware of the Loch - a sparkle glimpsed through foliage, or a sudden expanse that takes your breath away, some swans sailing peacefully by, or the soft metallic glimmer on a grey day. The water birds quite often step ashore and in the spring bring their young along too.

This book is a collection of recipes each of which has as a keynote ingredient something which grows in Dr Neil's Garden. This has been interpreted quite widely to include both wild and cultivated plants, and also honey from the bees which forage there. Included too are some of the tastier birds which visit the garden, and also rabbit. It must immediately be said that we do not in fact eat any of our visitors, and wildlife is generally encouraged. An exception is the rabbit whose voraciousness in the matter of young plants means that we do our utmost to keep him and all his tribe firmly outside the boundary.

Dr Neil's is an ornamental and not a productive garden. However, even without the vegetables and fruit trees of the domestic garden, there is still much of interest for the cook. We have included edible flowers, leaves, berries and funghi. Herbs are grown for sale in the Nursery, and we have made much use of these. All ingredients can easily be found either in your own or your neighbour's garden, growing wild in the countryside, or can be obtained commercially. In some cases - watercress for instance - the commercial variety is to be preferred to the wild, as it will have been grown under safe conditions. Mushrooms too, from the wild, should be viewed with caution, unless you are very sure of what you are doing. Botanical names of all plants (although not of all edible mushrooms) have been given as an aid to identification, but no further identifying details have been included as that is rather beyond the scope of this book. In particular the illustrations are not to be taken as a guide to identification. If you are at all in doubt, choose something else to cook! Remember too that insecticides and fungicides, unless specifically designed for food use, render plants unsuitable for eating.

SJM
Duddingston, Edinburgh 2006

DR NEIL'S GARDEN - A POTTED HISTORY

For more than 30 years, the people of Edinburgh, and literally thousands more from almost every corner of Britain and nation on the globe, have been visiting Dr Neil's Garden at Duddingston. Many visitors have come during an open day on behalf of the Scotland's Gardens Scheme (a few dozen on a wet Saturday, many hundreds on a sunny day - we've topped the thousand for a weekend on a couple of occasions), or the MS Therapy Centre, or have even come to watch a Festival Fringe performance. Add to that all the couples and their guests who have had their wedding photographs taken in the garden, the TV audiences who saw BBC Scotland's Beechgrove Garden or Channel 4's Garden Club in the 1980s and 1990s, or who were given a private tour with a local resident, and you will begin to understand how immensely proud I am that my parents' efforts have touched the lives of so many people.

I'd like to put on record here just a few of the events that lead to the creation of what Mum rather grandly called The Garden for Posterity. Andrew Jardine Neil (1921-2005) and Agnes Emily ('Nancy') Russell (1919-2005) first met as teenagers. Both grew up in Morningside, and they fell in love as medical students during the Second World War. On graduation, Dad joined the Royal Navy Reserves as a surgeon lieutenant on minesweepers in the Far East, while Mum trained in the clinics of Merseyside's dockland and elsewhere. They married on 12 April 1947 and, just before the establishment of the NHS, bought the general practice at Wolseley Gardens, Jock's Lodge.

From an unknown date, but certainly before I was born in 1955, they kept a large allotment garden at Morningside, near 'Holy Corner'. Dad was also a member of the Scottish Orchid Society, and through its members developed ties with the Royal Scottish Botanic Gardens.

However, in 1962 or '63, they were moved on so that a car park could be built. They were frantically searching for a home for their plants until a patient - who happened to be the Session Clerk at Duddingston Kirk - offered them the use of a piece of very overgrown glebe land, reached through the manse garden. Dennis White, in Exploring Old Duddingston and Portobello (Mainstream Publishing, 1990) identifies this land as part of an orchard and grass yard in a deed of 1586; there may have been a dovecote where Thomson's Tower was built in 1825. The tower - the restoration of which is at last a real possibility - is linked to the first written rules of curling, and was the studio of the artist the Rev John Thomson, who collaborated with J M W Turner as an illustrator, and with Sir Walter Scott.

For a few years, the doctors grew mostly potatoes and summer fruit bushes, but very quickly they began to develop a passion for alpine plants and primulae, heathers, azaleas, and cypresses (some plants were brought back thoroughly illegally from Spain and Greece), and the creation of this very special garden began. Success was hard won. Gardening was frequently done after evening surgery, by torchlight, and irrespective of the weather. I loved to help on the manual labouring side, as did a hardy band of friends and patients, but the garden's unique character was due entirely to my parents' inspiration and determination.

In 1975 the garden won an award from the British Tourist Authority during European Architectural Heritage Year, another from the Conservation Foundation in '84, and another in '86 in the Garden of the Year Competition organised by B&Q and the Sunday Express. In 1992, the Royal Caledonian Horticultural Society presented my parents each with The Queen Elizabeth the Queen Mother Medal in Horticulture, the first time that it had been awarded to amateur gardeners, or jointly.

In 1997, Dr Neil's Garden Trust was formed, with funding from the National Trust for Scotland, in order to take over the running of the garden, and to safeguard its future. Tell your friends about us, and help us to make Dr Neil's truly *A Garden for Posterity*.

Nigel Neil, Hon. President, Dr Neil's Garden Trust
Lancaster, July 2006

GARDENER'S NOTE

I first visited the garden with a friend who lived just across the road in Old Church Lane. She had been given a key by the Neils and, as it was a time in my life when I needed to make a career change, was trying to persuade me that I should consider gardening. My answer then was that I loved it too much to consider it as a career.

Some years later, after I'd trained at horticultural college, the same friend mentioned that the Neils, who were quite elderly by then, needed help in the garden and would I like to meet them. And so it began, this great adventure, at first for one day a week.

My first impressions were that the garden was fantastic, in a beautiful position, with some really choice specimen trees and plants. It was a magical place, unfolding in layers before you as you moved through it, but it was very 'mature', top heavy with trees that made it quite dark, and some plantings had suffered as a result. The Neils clearly did need help with the work load.

Early on in the development they had decided that they wanted an evergreen garden, one that would always have the feeling of being alive, even through the coldest darkest months. As a result the garden is full of the different hues and textures of conifers, the species *Juniperus pendula*, *Chamaecyparis macrocarpa* and *Abies concolor* being good examples.

They had also planted many heathers, hardy and with good all year value, hybrid rhododendrons and azaleas to add colour in the spring, and once the shelter belts had developed, magnolias and Japanese acers to complete the picture. All of these give the impression of an acid soil, but to my surprise the soil seems to be pretty neutral all over the garden, so in the autumn I apply loads of leaf mould and in the spring sequestrene by the bucketful.

When you first enter the garden, the ground falls away from you towards the loch, which is glimpsed through mature trees. Paths lead away in front and to the right, through the scree and on to the pond, or along the church wall and into the meadow garden. All paths lead down to the lochside eventually. The joy of the garden is the journey through it, along small winding paths, up and down steps, passing alpines in the scree, the herbaceous border, a riot of pinks, yellows and purples in August - and a wonderful example of Nancy Neil at her most exuberant, the shady border, the herb garden, two ponds, mature acers, specimen trees, azaleas and rhododendrons. Because the Neils began at the beginning (quite literally) and then gradually moved outwards from there, with no overall plan and dealing with problems as they presented themselves, the result is a garden with a very natural sense of movement.

As time goes on the garden continues to develop in both its form and its function. Plantings wear out and have to be replaced, crumbling walls and paths have to be re-built, vistas have to be maintained as trees and shrubs seek to encroach upon them. Space must be found for exciting new colours and textures.

The use of the garden changes also and we now encourage a wide range of visitors by having an open door policy which means that the garden can be visited any day of the year. It is used by local nursery schools as an educational resource and by art groups as a location for landscape studies. Newlyweds pose for their wedding photos in the garden and diverse groups use it as a place to get together and relax.

This wonderful garden, full of water, wind and birds, is a harmonious place, a peaceful place, but above all, a welcoming place. Come and see.

Claudia Pottier, Gardener, Dr Neil's Garden
Duddingston, August 2006

ANGELICA
Angelica archangelica

Mary, Queen of Scots is reputed to have introduced angelica to Scotland, and though it was almost certainly known long before that, at least to the monastic communities where it would have been grown for apothecary purposes, she may well have been responsible for popularising its culinary use.

CANDIED ANGELICA

    Angelica stems
    Caster sugar

Choose narrow, young stems and cut them into short lengths. Cook in boiling water until tender and then drain well. Weigh the angelica and layer it in a dish with an equal weight of caster sugar. Cover with a cloth and set aside for 1-2 days or until the sugar has dissolved. Transfer the angelica and sugar to a pan and heat gently until the liquid has almost evaporated (or if your quantity is small, just separate the pieces and place the dish in a low oven). Finish the drying process by spreading the angelica on a wire rack over a baking tray and leave in a warm place or low oven for 1-2 days. Store in an air-tight container.

CREAM CHEESE WITH ANGELICA
This is a recipe of Elizabeth David's from *Summer Cooking*.

    450g cream cheese
    90g caster sugar
    2 egg whites
    Candied angelica, chopped finely

Stir the cheese together with the sugar. Whip the egg whites until stiff and incorporate gently into the mixture. Add angelica to taste and put the whole into a muslin-lined sieve over a bowl to drain for a few hours. Chill before serving with some fresh cream, if you like, and perhaps a small crisp biscuit. Serves 8.

ANGELICA LIQUEUR

This recipe is based on one of Geraldene Holt's in *French Country Kitchen*.

> 60g young stems of fresh angelica, cut in short lengths
> ¼ teaspoon ground cinnamon
> ¼ teaspoon ground nutmeg
> 1¼ litre brandy
> 900g sugar
> 500ml bottled water

Put the angelica into a large Kilner jar or other glass vessel which can be sealed. Add the spices and the alcohol. Seal up and leave for four days. Then put the sugar and water in a large pan and dissolve slowly before raising the heat to bring to the boil and simmer for four minutes. When cool add to the angelica mixture. Seal again and leave for two months, and then strain through a fine muslin into smaller bottles.

BAY
Laurus nobilis

GRILLED BABY LEEKS
This recipe comes from Geraldene Holt's *A Taste of Herbs*.

250-350g baby leeks
12 or more bay leaves
60g butter
Finely grated zest of half an orange

Place the bay leaves in the basket of a steamer pan, and lay the leeks on top of them. Steam for 5-10 minutes until tender. Lift the leeks out and arrange them side by side in an oven-proof dish. Melt the butter with the zest and brush some over the leeks. Place under a pre-heated grill for 3 minutes or so until starting to brown. Spoon the remaining orange butter over them and serve. Serves 3-4.

ONION GRATIN
Marlena Spieler gives this recipe in her *Beggars' Banquets*.

10 medium onions
6-7 bay leaves
Salt, black pepper and nutmeg
284ml cream

Skin the onions but leave them whole. Simmer in water with salt and the bay leaves for 20 minutes. Drain and when cool enough, slice the onions into 1cm slices. Place in a shallow oven dish with a sprinkling of nutmeg, salt and pepper. Spoon over the cream and bake at 190°C, 375°F, Gas 5 for about an hour until crusty on top. Grind some black pepper over the dish. Good with roast or grilled lamb. Serves 4-6.

BAY ROAST POTATOES
Sue Lawrence recommended this recipe in her column in *Scotland on Sunday*.

1¼ kg potatoes
2 tablespoons olive oil (or 3 of goose fat)
50g butter, if you are using olive oil
6-8 fresh bay leaves

Peel the potatoes and cut into halves or quarters. Boil for 5 minutes with a little salt, and then drain and dry them well, over gentle heat if necessary. Heat the goose fat, or the olive oil with the butter, by placing the roasting tin in the hot oven, and then add the potatoes and the bay leaves. Season with salt and pepper and roast for approximately an hour at 190°C, 375°F, Gas 5. Remember to turn and baste them from time to time. Serves 6-8.

BAKED CUSTARD WITH BAY

450ml milk
450ml single cream
1 tablespoon granulated sugar
4-5 bay leaves
3 whole eggs and 3 yolks

Warm the milk, cream and sugar together with the bay leaves until the sugar is dissolved and then allow to cool a little. Whisk the eggs and extra yolks lightly, and then pour the warm milk on to them, stirring all the while. Strain the mixture into a buttered dish, or into individual ramekins. Place the dish or dishes into a shallow pan of warm water and bake at 190°C, 375°F, Mark 5 for about 40 minutes until set. Individual custards may take less time to cook. Chill before serving. Serves 6.

BAY LEAF MEATBALLS
This recipe is from Jill Dupleix's column in *The Times*.

100g breadcrumbs, made from day-old bread
500g minced chicken or turkey
50g Parmesan cheese, grated
1-2 cloves garlic, crushed
2 tablespoons finely chopped parsley
1-2 tablespoons lemon juice
Grated zest of 2 lemons
Sea salt and pepper
20 fresh bay leaves
Olive oil
20 cocktail sticks

Heat the oven to 200°C, 400°F, Gas 6. Mix the bread, meat, cheese, garlic, parsley, lemon juice, zest and seasoning. If you have added all the lemon juice and the mixture still seems dry, add a little milk. Using your hands form the mixture into balls about the size of a walnut. Lightly brush both sides of the bay leaves with olive oil and then bend a leaf around each meatball and secure with a cocktail stick. Bake the meatballs for 20 minutes until lightly browned and cooked through. The bay leaves should not be eaten and you may prefer to remove them before serving. Serves 4.

BOUQUET GARNI

Take a bay leaf or two, a few sprigs of thyme and some stalks of parsley in what proportion you please, and using some fine string, tie them together. You can add orange peel, cloves, celery or other herbs to taste. If you leave a long end to the string it will be easier to retrieve the bouquet at the end of cooking. If you have to use dried herbs, tie them into a small piece of muslin.

PANNACOTTA WITH BAY

125ml full cream milk
375ml single cream
50g caster sugar
A few drops vanilla essence
4 bay leaves
½ a sachet of powdered gelatine, softened in 2
    tablespoons of cold water

Put the milk, cream, sugar, vanilla and bay leaves into a small
pan and heat very gently for 10 minutes. Remove from the heat
and stir in the softened gelatine until it is completely dissolved.
When cool, remove the bay leaves and strain the mixture into
lightly oiled ramekin dishes or cups. Cover them with clingfilm
and chill for several hours or overnight. They will keep well for
a day or two in the fridge. Serve them either in their little pots
or dip the moulds into hot water for 10 seconds or so and turn
out onto flat plates and garnish with a little fruit or fruit sauce.
Serves 4.

BRAMBLE
Rubus fruticosus

BRAMBLE CURD
This recipe is from Joy Spoczynska's *The Wildfoods Cookbook*.

450g brambles
Juice of 1 lemon
340g caster sugar
120g butter
3 eggs

Wash the berries and without any further water cook in a heavy pan over a low heat until soft. Sieve to remove the pips. Put the berry pulp into the top of a double boiler (or a bowl fitted over an ordinary pan) together with the lemon juice, the butter and the sugar. Heat the water in the lower pan to a brisk simmer, and stir the curd with a wooden spoon until all the sugar is dissolved and the butter has blended into the mixture. Now beat the eggs and strain them into the mixture, stirring from time to time until the curd thickens sufficiently. Pot into sterilised jars. This is good on scones or toast.

BRAMBLE AND APPLE PIE

65g butter
1 teaspoon icing sugar
125g plain flour, sifted
1 egg yolk
60g demerara sugar
250g brambles
450g cooking apples
3-4 teaspoons rosewater

Mix the flour and the icing sugar and then rub in the butter (or use a processor). Work in the egg yolk and if necessary a little chilled water to make a stiff dough. Chill for half an hour. Peel, core and chop up the apples. Put half the chopped apple into a pie dish c.20cm diameter. Add the brambles, sugar and rosewater, and then finally the remaining apple. Roll out the pastry until you have a circle a little larger than your dish. Place the dish on the pastry and use as a guide to cut the pastry for the top. Use the trimmings to make an extra layer just on the rim, sticking it down with a little water. Moisten this rim of pastry with water and press the pastry circle to it. Make a small hole on the top for steam to escape and cook for 35 minutes at 190°C, 375° F, Gas 5. Serves 6.

BRAMBLE SYLLABUB
Claire Macdonald (www.claire-macdonald.com) gives this recipe in her *Seasonal Cooking*.

   450g brambles
   60-90g caster sugar
   212ml double cream
   3 tablespoons dry white wine

Rinse the berries and without further liquid cook gently in a heavy pan with a lid until the juice begins to run and the berries are just soft. Add the smaller quantity of sugar and stir until dissolved. Remove six good berries now for decoration if you wish. Purée the remainder in a blender and then sieve to remove the seeds. Leave to cool. Whip the cream with the white wine until just holding its shape and then fold the purée through it. Taste for sweetness and add more sugar if necessary. Divide the mixture between six ramekins or, preferably, glasses and top with the reserved berries. Chill for an hour or so. Lavender shortbread (p. 40) is particularly delicious with this. Serves 6.

BRAMBLE WHISKY
This recipe is given by Prue Coats in *The Poacher's Cookbook*,
from Merlin Unwin Books.

1¾ kg brambles
225g sugar
1 bottle whisky

Place fruit, sugar and whisky in a large screw top jar. Shake the
jar every day or two until the sugar has completely dissolved,
and then place the jar in a dark cupboard for 3 months or until
the whisky has turned a deep purple colour. Then strain the
liquid and decant into bottles. Best kept for a year before
drinking.

The brambles will have lost some colour but can be cooked
with apples in a pie, or sieved and served as a sauce with
vanilla ice-cream. Or you could use them to replace the fresh
brambles in the next recipe, in which case omit the brandy.

AUTUMN FRUIT SALAD

4 ripe plums
2 large Williams pears
200g brambles
Grated zest of 1 orange
50g caster sugar
2 tablespoons apple or pear brandy (optional)

Wash and dry the fruit. Peel the pears and divide them and the
plums into quarters, removing the seeds and stones. Put them
into a bowl with the brambles and scatter the orange zest and
the caster sugar over the fruit. Then add the brandy and stir
gently through the fruit mixture. Cover and chill for an hour or
two, and then serve with thick cream or yoghurt. Serves 4.

18

ELDER
Sambucus nigra

ELDERBERRY ICE CREAM
This comes from *The Wildfoods Cookbook* by Joy Spoczynska.

450g elderberries
175g caster sugar
50g icing sugar
275ml double cream
2 egg whites

Remove the major stalks from the berries, wash them, and place them in a pan without further water. Heat gently to break up the berries and make the juice run. Bring just up to the boil, adding a very little water if it seems too dry, simmer for 1 minute, and then leave to cool a little. Put the fruit through a blender, and then through a sieve to remove the seeds. Stir in the caster sugar, making sure it is completely dissolved. Allow to cool completely. Whip the cream with the sifted icing sugar until just thick enough to stand in peaks and then fold the purée gently into the cream. Whisk the egg whites until stiff and fold into the mixture. Turn into a covered container and freeze. Serves 6-8.

ELDERBERRY JELLIES
This is a recipe of Geraldene Holt's from her book *French Country Kitchen*.

225g elderberries
275ml red wine
60-90g sugar
2 teaspoons powdered gelatine
4 tablespoons lemon juice

Rinse the berries in cold water and remove the larger stalks. The tiny stalks will be strained out later. Cover the fruit with the wine, cover and leave in a cool place overnight. The next day turn the wine and fruit into a non-aluminium pan, add the sugar and break up the fruit with a potato masher. Slowly bring the mixture almost to the boil. Taste for sweetness at this point, bearing in mind the lemon juice to come, and add sugar if necessary. Strain through a muslin-lined sieve and allow to cool.
Put the lemon juice in a small bowl or cup and sprinkle on the gelatine. Place the bowl in a shallow pan of simmering water and stir until the gelatine is completely dissolved. Stir the gelatine into the fruity wine, and then divide the mixture between four glasses. Leave to set. Serve lightly chilled with perhaps a little cream. Serves 4.

ELDERBERRY AND APPLE CRUMBLE

300g cooking apples
125g elderberries
150g soft brown sugar
120g flour
60g caster sugar
80g butter

Wash and then strip the elderberries from their stalks as thoroughly as patience permits. Peel, core and cut up the apples and place all the fruit in an oven-proof dish. Sprinkle with the soft brown sugar. For the crumble mix the dry ingredients together, then rub in the butter. Spread the mixture over the fruit and pat down lightly. Bake at 200°C, 400°F, Gas 6 for about 35 minutes until the top is lightly browned. Serves 3-4.

ELDERBERRY CHUTNEY

450g elderberries
1 medium onion, roughly chopped
250g raisins
300ml vinegar
100g sugar
1 teaspoon salt
1 teaspoon ground ginger
½ teaspoon cayenne pepper
2 teaspoons mustard seeds, crushed
1 teaspoon allspice

Strip the berries from the stalks and mince or process them with the onion and raisins. Put the processed ingredients into a non-aluminium pan and add the vinegar, sugar, salt and all the spices. Simmer gently, stirring from time to time, and when thickened to your taste, spoon into hot sterilised jars and seal.

ELDERFLOWER SYRUP

175g granulated sugar
Pared rind and juice of 2 lemons
3 handfuls elderflower

Put the sugar and lemon rind in a pan with 600ml water and let the sugar dissolve over gentle heat. Then increase the heat and boil fast for 5 minutes. Take the pan off the hob and add the lemon juice and the elderflowers. When the syrup is completely cool, strain it through a sieve. If not for immediate use, decant it into a bottle with a screwtop or a cork and keep in the fridge.

Elderflower syrup can be used to make fruit salad, and is particularly sympathetic with strawberries alone - macerate the berries for 2-3 hours in the syrup. It is delicious also with dessert crêpes (you can add some tiny florets of fresh elder to the crêpe mixture if you like), and diluted with chilled sparkling water makes a refreshing summer drink. It can also be used as the basis of a muscat-flavoured sorbet.

ELDERFLOWER SORBET

Elderflower syrup, made with 600 ml water as above
1-2 egg whites

Put the cold syrup in a covered container and place in the freezer. As it freezes keep scraping the frozen parts from the sides of the container and stirring into the more liquid part of the mixture. When you have a fairly solid slush, add 1-2 egg whites, beaten stiff, and return to freezer. Serves 4.

ELDERFLOWER ICE CREAM
This is from *The Wildfoods Cookbook* by Joy Spoczynska.

8 elderflower heads
75g caster sugar
200ml full cream milk
2 lemons
142ml single cream
1 egg white

Strip the elderflowers from the heads, discarding all stalks. Bring the flowers to the boil in the milk, and then add the caster sugar and the grated rind and juice of the lemons. Reduce the heat and simmer very gently for about 10 minutes, taking care not to reach a boil again. Ensure that all the sugar has dissolved, then strain through a muslin-lined sieve and allow to cool. When almost cold, add the cream, stirring it in thoroughly. Place in a covered container and freeze for about an hour. The time taken will depend on your freezer, but when the mixture is no longer liquid but still not hard, beat the egg white until it is standing in peaks and fold it into the elderflower mixture, distributing it evenly. Return the mixture to the freezer. This makes a very light, refreshing ice cream. Serves 4.

STRAWBERRY AND ELDERFLOWER JAM
This delicious recipe is from *Seasonal Cooking* by Claire Macdonald (www.claire-macdonald.com).

1½ kg strawberries
1½ kg granulated sugar
Juice of 1 lemon
Handful of redcurrants (optional)
3-4 handfuls of elderflowers

Hull the strawberries, leaving them whole, and put them into a preserving pan or large saucepan with the sugar, lemon juice and the redcurrants, if you have them, with their stalks removed. Carefully strip the tiny elderflowers from their stalks and add them all to the contents of the pan. Cover the pan and leave in a warm place for a few hours.

Then put the pan over a gentle heat, stirring until the sugar has completely dissolved. Raise the heat and boil fast for 10-15 minutes and test for a set. Remember always to take the pan off the heat while you do this. If necessary boil the strawberry mixture for another 5 minutes until the surface of a few drops of the jam chilled on a plate will wrinkle when pushed with a hopeful finger.

Leave the jam to cool in the pan for 20 minutes or so, and then decant into warmed jars and seal.

GOOSEBERRY AND ELDERFLOWER JELLY

Gooseberries
Sugar
Elderflowers

Wash the berries, but there is no need to top and tail them. Put into a pan with about 150ml water to every 450g of fruit. Simmer gently until the fruit breaks up and the juice is flowing. Strain through a jelly bag or a muslin placed in a sieve. Press the fruit gently to release the juice. Measure the juice and weigh out 350g sugar to each 600ml of juice. Bring the juice to the boil, add the sugar, stir to dissolve, and continue to boil until setting point is reached (221°F, or until a drop sets on a chilled plate). Have ready a generous bunch of elderflowers tied up in a piece of muslin, and, with the pan off the heat, swirl the elderflowers round in the jelly until the flavour is to your liking. Be sure to put your tiny samples on your chilled plate first or you will burn your tongue! Ladle the jelly into clean, warmed jars and seal.

GARLIC
Allium roseum

Wild garlic is milder than commercial garlic, so if you want to try the wild version you may need to adjust the quantities in these recipes which are based on garden or farmed garlic. You can use the leaves and flowers as well as the bulbs of wild garlic.

ALMOND SOUP WITH GARLIC
This excellent soup comes from *The Flavours of Andalucia* by Elisabeth Luard.

> 200g blanched almonds
> 6 tablespoons olive oil
> 1 slice of stale bread
> 12 garlic cloves, roughly chopped
> 2-3 sprigs of parsley, roughly chopped
> 1 teaspoon cumin seeds
> A pinch of saffron threads
> Salt and pepper

Warm the olive oil in a small frying-pan and add the garlic. Cook gently until just coloured and then remove the garlic and put on one side. Increase the heat a trifle and put into the garlic-flavoured oil the almonds, the bread cut into cubes and the parsley, and cook gently until the nuts have taken on some colour. Put the nuts, bread, parsley, any remaining oil and the reserved garlic into a saucepan with the cumin and saffron and add 900ml water. Stir to mix and then bring slowly to the boil. Simmer for 5-10 minutes, then allow to cool for a few minutes before whizzing the lot in a food processor or liquidiser. Return to the pan and add salt and pepper to taste. Serve with toasted flaked almonds or with croûtons. Serves 4-6.

CHICKEN LEGS WITH WHOLE CLOVES OF GARLIC

This and the next recipe are from Geraldene Holt's *French Country Kitchen*. This one has been adapted slightly.

4 legs of chicken, fairly large
30g butter
Salt and black pepper
8 slices smoked streaky bacon
16-20 cloves garlic, unpeeled
2 glasses rosé wine and 1 of light stock or water

Skin the meat and lightly brown it in the butter. Season each leg and wrap two slices of bacon around each. Place the wrapped legs in a roasting tin and add the cloves of garlic, tucking them close to the meat. Roast at 190°C, 375°F, Gas 5 for 45-50 minutes, basting with the cooking juices every 15 minutes or so. The meat is cooked when, inserting a sharp knife into the thickest part, the juice runs clear. Put the meat and the garlic on a serving dish to keep warm and make a gravy by pouring off the fat from the tin, adding the wine and stock, and boiling to reduce the quantity by half. Taste and add seasoning if necessary. Serves 4.

GOATS' CHEESE WITH GARLIC

100g soft goats' cheese
2-3 tablespoons olive oil
2-3 teaspoons white wine vinegar
1-2 cloves garlic, crushed
Salt, black pepper and cayenne pepper

Mash the cheese in a bowl and gradually add the other ingredients. Adjust the seasonings to your taste. This is excellent with baked potatoes, or you could thin it slightly with some crème fraîche and use it as a dip. Serves 4.

CHEESY GARLIC BREAD

This is a variation of ordinary garlic bread. With the addition of cheese it is more substantial, and, accompanied by a bowl of soup, will make a satisfying meal.

1 short baguette
1 garlic clove, crushed
30g butter, softened
A little smoked paprika
Chopped herbs
125g raclette or any cheese that will melt
Black pepper, freshly ground
1 tablespoon olive oil

Heat the oven to 180°C, 350°F, Gas 4. Cut the baguette into thick slices, leaving them still joined at the base. Mix the butter with the crushed garlic, the paprika pepper and the herbs, and spread some on each cut face of bread. Cut the cheese into slices, and then wedge them into the cuts in the bread. Dribble a little oil over the top and grind some black pepper over all. Wrap in foil. Bake for 15 minutes until the cheese is starting to melt and eat while warm. Serves 2-3.

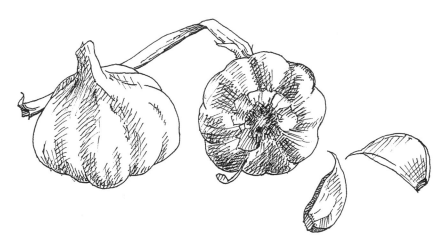

GERANIUM
Pelargonium capitatum

GERANIUM CREAM

Elizabeth David gives this recipe in her inspirational *Summer Cooking*.

284ml double cream
180-200g cream cheese, ideally Isigny or Chambourcy
4 tablespoons sugar
2 sweet-scented geranium leaves

Put the cream into a double saucepan, or a bowl over a pan, and add the sugar and the whole geranium leaves. Let the cream get thoroughly hot, but do not let it boil. Leave to cool with the leaves still in the cream. Then soften the cheese by beating it a little, and slowly add the flavoured cream, still with the leaves. Cover and leave in the fridge for 12 hours. Remove the leaves just before serving. This can be eaten on its own, or is delicious accompanying fresh brambles. Serves 8.

APPLE AND GERANIUM JELLY

1½ kg cooking apples
Juice of 1 lemon
Sugar
Geranium leaves, washed and dried

Wash the apples removing any damaged portions, and then cut them into thick slices without peeling or coring. Put them in a pan with the lemon juice and sufficient cold water to cover. Simmer until the apples are completely soft and the liquid is reduced to about two thirds. Strain the pulp through a muslin-lined sieve or a jelly-bag. Leave to drip for several hours - overnight if you like. Then measure the extract and put it in a capacious pan with 450g sugar to 600ml extract. Bring slowly to the boil, stirring until the sugar has dissolved. Once the mixture is boiling add the geranium leaves - approximately 12g of leaves to each 600ml of extract. Boil rapidly until setting point is reached. Remove the leaves (this is simpler if you have used a few large leaves rather than many small ones), ladle the jelly into warmed jars and cover in the usual way.

This is an excellent preserve in its own right, with scones perhaps, or with toast, but it is also very good used in the next two recipes.

BAKED APPLES WITH GERANIUM LEAVES
This recipe comes from *Rosemary Hemphill's Herb Collection*, published by Aurum Press.

    4 cooking apples
    4 teaspoons apple jelly, preferably geranium flavoured
    4 geranium leaves, each with an inch or so of stem
    Butter
    1 tablespoon sugar

Wash the apples, cut a little of the skin away from the top and core. Put a little butter into the cavities, and add 1 teaspoon of apple jelly to each. Top each apple with a leaf. Stand the apples in a baking dish with a little water and bake in a medium to hot oven (200°C, 400°F, Gas 6) until just soft. Pour off the liquid into a small saucepan, add 1 tablespoon sugar and boil for a few minutes to reduce and thicken. Pour the syrup over the apples and eat them hot with some thick cream or ice cream. The leaves, crisp and blackened, may be used as a garnish. Serves 4.

ROSE GERANIUM SPONGE CAKE

This recipe also comes from *Rosemary Hemphill's Herb Collection*, published by Aurum Press.

4 eggs, separated
170g caster sugar
175g self-raising flour
30g cornflour
20g butter, melted
4 tablespoons hot water
Rose geranium leaves, washed and dried
Pinch salt

Put 2 or 3 geranium leaves to infuse in the hot water, and keep the water warm. Grease and lightly flour two 20cm cake tins, and then cover the bases with more geranium leaves. Remove the stems completely so that they lie as flat as possible. Separate the egg whites and beat until stiff. Gradually add the sugar, beating until it is dissolved. Break up the egg yolks and gently add to the meringue. Sift the flour, cornflour and salt, and fold into the egg mixture. Add the melted butter and the hot water, strained, folding in gently, and then divide into the prepared tins. Bake in a fairly hot oven 200°C, 400°F, Gas 6 on the bottom shelf for 20 minutes. When done, turn out onto a wire tray to cool. Then carefully remove the geranium leaves and sandwich the cakes together with the apple geranium jelly above, or with whipped cream faintly sweetened, or a combination. Double cream whipped stiff with some finely chopped stem ginger stirred into it is particularly good.

HONEY

Hives are kept in the adjoining field and bees are constant visitors to Dr Neil's Garden. Pat McErlean sells his honey at Open Weekends in the Garden.

HONEY AND MUSTARD GLAZED DUCK
This recipe is reproduced by kind permission of Sainsbury's Supermarkets Ltd.

　　4 skinless duck breast fillets
　　2 teaspoons clear honey
　　2 teaspoons wholegrain mustard
　　1 teaspoon ground cinnamon
　　1 teaspoon grated root ginger

Preheat the oven to 190°C, 375°F, Gas 5. Trim any sinew away from the duck and pat dry with kitchen towel. Season with salt and freshly ground pepper. Mix the honey, mustard, cinnamon and ginger together in a small bowl and then spread the mixture all over the duck pieces. Place them not touching each other in a small roasting tin, and cook on a high shelf for 20-25 minutes. Allow to rest out of the oven for 5 minutes before serving with boiled rice or new potatoes. Serves 4.

ONION AND HONEY SAUCE
This recipe comes from Arto der Haroutunian's *North African Cookery*. Ras-el-hanout is a spice blend which can be purchased already mixed.

　　3 tablespoons oil
　　450g onions, finely chopped
　　1½ tablespoons ras-el-hanout
　　1-2 tablespoons honey

Put the onions in a small saucepan and cover with water. Bring to the boil and simmer for a few minutes until soft. Drain the onions and put back in the pan with the oil, spices and half a teaspoon of salt. Cook gently for 2-3 minutes, stirring frequently. Add the honey and allow to simmer for another couple of minutes. Serve hot with gammon, or with sausages. Serves 4-6.

HONEY AND WALNUT ICE CREAM
This delicious confection comes from *Ice Creams and Sorbets* by Jill Norman.

300ml milk
75g walnuts, chopped coarsely
125g honey
3 egg yolks
2 tablespoons brandy (optional)
142ml double cream

Spread the chopped nuts out in a small baking tray and put in a moderate oven for 5-10 minutes. Bring the milk to the boil, then remove the pan from the heat, add the walnuts and leave to infuse for 10 minutes. Heat the honey almost to boiling point. Whisk the egg yolks in a bowl, and then, still whisking add the hot honey. Continue beating for 3-4 minutes. Either transfer the mixture to a double boiler, or place the bowl over a pan of barely simmering water. Add the milk and walnuts to the mixture and stir over low heat until the mixture starts to thicken, coating the back of the spoon. Do not let it boil. Remove from the heat and cool. Then stir in the brandy and the lightly whipped double cream. Pour into a lidded container and freeze. Stir vigorously twice during the freezing process. Serves 4.

SOLOMON'S DELIGHT

16 dried figs
3 teaspoons rosewater
1 teaspoon sugar
90g honey
600ml single cream
8 egg yolks
Generous pinch saffron strands

Soak the figs for an hour or two in water to cover with 2 teaspoons of rosewater added. Then simmer them for 10 minutes in the soaking water with a teaspoon of sugar. Remove from the heat and after 5 minutes, add another teaspoon of rosewater to the liquid. Cover and leave to infuse. When cool, drain and cut each fig into three, removing the hard stalk, and divide the pieces between 8 buttered ramekin dishes.

To make the custard, weigh the honey into a generously sized bowl. Beat the cream and the yolks into the honey, and then add the saffron. Place the bowl over a pan of barely simmering water (the bowl should not touch the water), or use a double boiler and cook, stirring all the time until the mixture is thick enough to coat the back of a spoon. Remove instantly from the heat and pour immediately into the prepared ramekin dishes. Stand the ramekins in a bain marie with hot water no more than half way up their sides. Bake in a low oven until just set - about 15-20 minutes at 150°C, 300°F, Gas 2. The tops should be lightly coloured, so give them a little longer if necessary. Chill before serving. These will keep quite well in the fridge for 24 hours or so. Serves 8.

HONEY TEABREAD
Margaret Costa gives this recipe in *Four Seasons Cookbook.*

350g plain flour
3 level teaspoons baking powder
½ level teaspoon bicarbonate of soda
1 teaspoon salt
Grated rind of 1 large orange
Juice of 3 oranges (300ml)
100ml honey
1 egg, beaten
60g chopped walnuts

Sift the dry ingredients together. Beat the butter and sugar together with the orange rind. Measure the honey (warming it slightly will make this easier) and mix it into the butter and sugar. Add the egg, stirring it in thoroughly. Add the flour a little at a time, alternating with additions of orange juice. You should have a thick batter mixture. Stir in the nuts and turn into one large or two smaller prepared loaf tins and bake for 50-60 minutes at 170°C, 325°F, Gas 3. Cool, and slice to serve.

HONEY AND CARDAMOM SAUCE

2 tablespoons honey
Zest of ½ orange
2 tablespoons orange juice
2 pods cardamom

Using a sharp knife, cut away the green husk of the cardamom pods, and with a pestle and mortar grind the black seeds finely. Put all the ingredients in a small pan and warm gently for a minute or two. Take off the heat and leave to infuse. This may be warmed again to serve. Good with vanilla ice cream or pannacotta, or with crêpes. Serves 2-4.

JAPONICA (FLOWERING QUINCE)
Chaenomeles japonica

The fruits of the flowering quince are commonly regarded as merely decorative, but, although you cannot eat them raw, cooked they are well worth the trouble.

GUINEA FOWL WITH QUINCE AND HONEY

This is adapted from a recipe in *The Poacher's Cookbook* by Prue Coats, published by Merlin Unwin Books.

50g butter
2 guinea fowl
4 rashers bacon, chopped
4 shallots, peeled and finely chopped
120g quince, peeled, cored and cut up
300ml stock
1 glass cider
Salt and pepper
1-2 tablespoons honey
2 tablespoons crème fraîche

Heat the butter in a heavy casserole and put in the birds, the bacon, shallots and quince. Cook for a minute or two to colour slightly, keeping everything moving around. Then pour in the stock and the cider and season with salt and pepper. Put the lid on the casserole and place in a preheated oven 180°C, 350°F, Gas 4 for 1½ hours or until tender. Carve the birds and then cover the meat and keep warm. Boil the sauce to reduce it and then add the honey a teaspoonful at a time to taste. Break down the fruit in the sauce with a potato masher, or, if you prefer it smoother, put it in the liquidiser. Reheat if necessary, and stir a little of it into the crème fraîche before adding the cream to the sauce. Arrange the meat on hot plates and spoon the sauce over it. Serves 4-6.

JAPONICA JAM

2kg japonica fruit
3½ litres water
Sugar
2 level teaspoons powdered cloves (or other spice)

Wash and slice the fruit (no need to peel), and put it into a pan with the water. Boil until the fruit is soft, and then sieve it. Weigh the pulp, and put it back in the pan with an equal weight of sugar. Bring slowly to the boil, stirring frequently. Add the spice and continue to boil until setting point is reached (221°F on a sugar thermometer). As soon as it jells, pour into hot, dry jars and cover immediately in the usual way.

JUNIPER
Juniperus communis

Juniper berries should be picked when they are blue. Dry them in a cool oven and store in small jars.

MARINADE FOR GAME

    2 glasses red wine
    4 tablespoons olive oil
    1 onion, sliced
    1 clove garlic
    6 juniper berries
    ¼ teaspoon chopped thyme
    4 black peppercorns, crushed

Mix all together. Instead of red wine, you could use white wine, cider or wine vinegar. You can add carrot and celery, other herbs - bay or rosemary perhaps - and spices. Soaking time can vary from an hour or so, to two or three days. Turn the meat in the marinade now and then.

POTATOES WITH JUNIPER
Joy Spoczynska gives this recipe in *The Wildfoods Cookbook*.

Parboil some new potatoes for about 5 minutes. Melt some butter with oil in a heavy frying pan and add the drained potatoes. Cook slowly, turning from time to time, until well coloured and soft in the middle. Towards the end of the cooking time add some crushed juniper berries, about 12 berries to 450g potatoes. Delicious with game.

WILD DUCK WITH JUNIPER

This is one of the many tempting recipes in *French Country Kitchen* by Geraldene Holt.

    1 wild duck
    1 carrot
    1 small onion
    1 stick of celery
    15-18 juniper berries
    200ml chicken or duck stock
    ½ wineglass gin
    45g butter
    Salt

Chop the vegetables and place in the roasting pan. Crush half of the juniper berries and place in the cavity of the duck. Sprinkle salt on the skin and place the bird on the bed of vegetables. Roast at 200°C, 400°F, Gas 6 for 45 minutes. Pour off any surplus fat and turn the bird breast side down. Return to the oven for a further 10 minutes, and then when the meat is cooked through, transfer to a dish and keep hot. Pour off the fat from the roasting tin and add the remaining juniper berries and the stock to it. Boil for 3-4 minutes and then strain the liquid into a jug, discarding the vegetables. Pour the gin into the pan and set light to it. Return the strained juices to the pan and simmer for 2 minutes stirring all the time. Turn the heat off and add the butter, cut into small pieces, and let it melt into the sauce. Carve the duck and serve on hot plates with the sauce. Serves 2-4.

LAVENDER
Lavandula

Lavender can be used fresh or dried. To dry, remove the tiny flowers (with the calyx) from the stem and spread out in shallow trays. Place the trays on top of the central heating boiler, or in the airing cupboard. Store the dried lavender in screwtop jars and keep away from the light.

DUCK BREASTS WITH LAVENDER AND THYME
This is based on a recipe in *Cooking with Flowers* by Jenny Leggatt.

2 tablespoons oil
4 duck breasts
8 small shallots, halved
1-2 tablespoons flour
225ml white wine
225ml duck or chicken stock
Salt and black pepper
4 sprigs of thyme
1½ tablespoons dried lavender
2 oranges

Heat the oven to 170°C, 325°F, Gas 3. In a heavy frying pan heat the oil with a knob of butter and brown the duck breasts in it. Transfer the meat in one layer to a casserole. Sauté the shallots for 2 minutes and add them. Sprinkle in enough flour to absorb the remaining fat in the frying pan (add a little more butter if necessary), and cook stirring for 2 minutes. Slowly, stirring all the time, add the wine and stock and bring to the boil. Season to taste. Stir in the thyme, lavender, and the zest and juice of 1 orange and pour over the duck breasts. Cover the casserole and cook in the oven for 30-40 minutes until the duck is tender. Transfer the breasts to a serving dish and if the sauce is too thin, reduce it to a thicker consistency by boiling for a few minutes. Pour the sauce over the meat and garnish with segments of orange and fresh lavender sprigs. Serves 4.

If you have some lavender sugar, made by storing caster sugar with some dried lavender in an airtight jar, you can use it to good effect in the following three recipes.

LAVENDER JELLY

200ml dry white wine
200ml unsweetened apple juice
2 tablespoons crème de cassis
50g sugar
2 tablespoons lemon juice
25g lavender
4 teaspoons gelatine
4 tablespoons water

Gently heat the white wine with the apple juice, crème de cassis, sugar and lemon juice. Turn the heat off, stir the lavender into the mixture, and leave, covered, to infuse for about 10 minutes. Put the measured water into a cup or small bowl and sprinkle the gelatine onto it. Allow to soften and then stand the cup in a shallow pan of simmering water until the gelatine is completely dissolved. Strain the lavender liquid, pressing the flowers to obtain maximum flavour. Add the dissolved gelatine, stir and strain again through a sieve lined with muslin. Decant into wineglasses or ramekins and leave to set. This makes a refreshing pudding either on its own, or with the addition of a little cream. Serves 6.

LAVENDER SHORTBREAD

> 250g plain flour
> 125g caster sugar
> 125g ground rice
> 1 tablespoon dried lavender
> 250g butter

Mix all the dry ingredients together and add the butter cut into small cubes. Either use your fingers to rub in the butter, or put the whole lot in a food processor until you have a crumbly mixture. Stir in the lavender and, using your knuckles, press the mixture into a shallow tin approx. 25 x 18cm. It should be pricked all over with a fork, but this is much more easily done after it has started to cohere, so do it after 10 or 15 minutes in the oven. Overall the shortbread needs about 1 hour at 160°C, 325°F, Gas 3 until faintly coloured. Mark it into squares when it comes out of the oven but let it firm up in the tin for a few minutes before separating the pieces and returning them, dusted with caster sugar, to a slightly cooler oven for another 10 minutes. Finally transfer them to a wire tray to cool completely.

LAVENDER MERINGUES

> 2 large egg whites
> 125g caster sugar
> ½ teaspoon vinegar
> 1 rounded tablespoon of dried lavender

Line the baking tray with non-stick baking paper or grease with butter and powder with flour. Whisk the egg whites until fairly stiff. Add some of the sugar and continue whisking and adding the sugar gradually until it is all used up. Fold in the vinegar and finally the lavender. Spoon or pipe the mixture onto the tray to make approximately 16 meringues. Cook at 130°C, 250°F, Gas 1 for 2 hours until crisp. Sometimes it is a good idea to turn the meringues over on the tray and give them another half hour or so in the oven to allow the bases to crisp. Serve with double cream whipped till stiff.

MARIGOLD
Calendula officinalis

Marigold petals can be used fresh or dried. Sometimes called Poor Man's Saffron, they are faintly spicy in flavour and have a good orange-yellow colour, though without the staining property of true saffron. Make sure you use the right kind of marigold - not the African marigold (*Tagetes*).

CHESTNUT AND MUSHROOM SOUP
This unusual soup comes from *Cooking with Flowers* by Jenny Leggatt.

 450g fresh chestnuts
 60g butter
 1 onion, finely chopped
 4 large field mushrooms, finely sliced
 150ml vegetable or chicken stock
 2 tablespoons dried marigold petals, and more for garnish
 Salt and pepper
 425ml full-cream milk

Pierce the chestnut shells with the point of a sharp knife and simmer them in water for 15 minutes to soften. Cool a little and peel them. (This is a fiddly and time-consuming job, so you may prefer to use ready prepared chestnuts. Try to avoid chestnut purée, however, which is rather too smooth.) Sauté the onion in the butter until it is soft but not coloured. Add the chestnuts and mushrooms and cook for a few minutes. Add the stock, marigold petals, milk and seasoning to taste. Simmer gently for 5 minutes. Put the soup through a blender or processor, but don't let it get too smooth. Return to the pan to reheat and serve garnished with marigold petals, and chopped parsley too if you like. Serves 4-6.

SWEETCORN AND MARIGOLD FRITTERS

100g canned sweetcorn, drained
100g self-raising flour, sifted
1 medium egg, beaten
2 tablespoons marigold petals
1 level teaspoon baking powder
3 tablespoons milk
2 teaspoons of finely chopped parsley

Put 75g of the sweetcorn in a food processor and add the flour, egg, marigold, baking powder, milk, parsley and a little seasoning. Process for 15 seconds or so until evenly mixed. Stir in the remaining sweetcorn and then turn the mixture onto a board and shape into four rounds about 10cm across. Heat some oil in a heavy frying-pan and cook the fritters for about 3 minutes each side until golden brown. Serve with a well-flavoured salad. Serves 4.

EGGS COOKED WITH MARIGOLD
This recipe is given in *The Gentle Art of Cookery* by Mrs C.F. Leyel and Miss Olga Hartley.

10-12 marigold heads
2 fresh eggs
Salt, pepper and nutmeg
2 slices of bread
A little milk

Tap the flower heads gently to get rid of any insects, and then chop the petals only. Blanch them briefly in boiling water. Put the eggs to poach in just simmering water, and while they are cooking sprinkle them thickly with the chopped petals and season them with nutmeg, salt and pepper. They should be poached very slowly. Meanwhile dip the slices of bread, both sides, briefly in the milk and fry to colour and crisp in some oil, or butter and oil. Sprinkle the croûtes with some more chopped petals and lay the eggs on top. Garnish with parsley and fresh marigold flowers. Serves 2.

CREAM CHEESE WITH MARIGOLD

225g soft cream cheese (low fat if you like)
1 tablespoon parsley, chopped
4 tablespoons marigold petals, chopped
Salt and black pepper and a pinch of nutmeg

Combine all the ingredients together thoroughly. Cover and chill until required. This can be served simply with bread or oatcakes, but it is also good as a starter with a tomato salad.

MARIGOLD RICE

350g Basmati rice, washed well in cold water
Petals from 12-16 marigold heads
Pinch nutmeg
2 cloves and a small piece of cinnamon
1-2 tablespoons olive oil
1 teaspoon salt

Measure 850ml water into a large pan of salted water to the boil and put in the rice, marigold petals, spices and salt. Bring to the boil, stir briskly, put the lid on the pan and turn the heat to the lowest setting. Cook for about 15 minutes and then test a grain for readiness. Replace the lid and leave off the heat for 10 minutes. Add the olive oil and stir it in gently with a fork. To serve, fish out the cloves and the cinnamon. A few fresh marigold petals at this stage looks pretty. Serves 4.

MINT
Mentha rotundifolia, spicata

MINT AND CUCUMBER SOUP
This useful recipe comes from *Cordon Bleu Cookery* by
Rosemary Hume and Muriel Downes.

900ml chicken stock
2 large cucumbers, peeled and cut into thick slices
1 small onion, chopped
30g butter
1 tablespoon flour
Salt and pepper
70ml cream
Chopped mint

Simmer the cucumber and onion in the stock for 15 to 20 minutes until soft. Rub through a sieve, or liquidise. In a clean pan
melt the butter, work in the flour gradually and then add the
cucumber liquid, slowly at first, stirring all the time. Stir until
boiling and simmer for 2 to 3 minutes. Take off the heat for a
minute or two, then stir in the cream and the chopped mint to
taste. Serves 4.

OMELETTE BERRICHONNE
This is Elizabeth David's recipe from *Summer Cooking*.

4 eggs
Salt and pepper
1 small leek, white part only, finely sliced
1 shallot, chopped
1 tablespoon cream
Chopped mint
Butter for frying

Start by softening the shallot without browning in a little butter, and set on one side. Beat the eggs with seasoning in a bowl. Make the pan quite hot and drop in the butter and swirl around. Add the eggs and immediately start lifting the set omelette at the edge to let the liquid egg run under. While it is still in the pan, scatter on the sliced leek, softened shallot and chopped mint, and sprinkle with the cream. Fold in three and serve. Serves 2.

CHICKEN WITH MINT AND GINGER
Josceline Dimbleby has kindly updated her recipe which appeared originally in *Favourite Food*.

6 joints chicken
2 tablespoons sunflower oil
5-6 stalks of mint, leaves stripped and chopped
2 teaspoons finely chopped rosemary
2 cloves of garlic
2-3 cm piece of root ginger, peeled and finely chopped
Salt, black pepper
100-175g brown chestnut mushrooms, sliced
Juice of 1 lemon
1 tablespoon honey
1 tablespoon extra virgin olive oil
Soy sauce

Heat the oven to 180°C, 350°F, Gas 4. Brown the chicken in the sunflower oil with a pat of butter. Transfer the pieces to an ovenproof dish. Sprinkle over the rosemary, garlic, ginger, salt and pepper. Arrange the mushrooms around the meat, spoon over the lemon juice, honey and olive oil, and add a generous sprinkling of soy sauce. Cover the dish with a lid or foil and cook in the oven for 1-1½ hours. Check once or twice that the chicken is still moist, and top up with a little stock or water if necessary. Sprinkle on the mint before serving. Serves 6.

CARROTS WITH MINT

450g small new carrots
2 cloves garlic, crushed
Handful of fresh mint leaves, chopped
Salt, black pepper
4 tablespoons oil
2 tablespoons white wine vinegar

Parboil the carrots for approximately 10 minutes - they should not be too soft - and drain them. Put them back in the pan with all the other ingredients. Cook gently, turning the carrots from time to time, for another 5 minutes. Hot, this is good with lamb, or serve it cold as salad. Serves 4-6.

ORANGE MINT FRUIT SALAD

This refreshing salad comes from *The Gentle Art of Cookery* by Mrs C.F. Leyel and Miss Olga Hartley, published by The Hogarth Press in 1925.

4 large oranges
1-2 tablespoons sugar (to taste)
2 tablespoons of finely chopped mint
1 tablespoon sherry
1 tablespoon lemon juice

With a sharp knife cut away all the skin and pith of the oranges. Then slice across into rounds and place in a dish. Sprinkle with the sugar, mint, sherry and lemon juice. Chill for a couple of hours and serve garnished with whole mint leaves. Serves 4.

MINT ICE CREAM

Katie Stewart gave this recipe in her column in *The Times*.

120g caster sugar
150ml water
1 teacupful applemint or spearmint leaves
Juice of ½ lemon
284ml double cream

Wash the mint leaves stripped from the stems and squeeze dry, and then place in the goblet of a liquidiser. Put the sugar and water in a small saucepan. Stir over low heat until the sugar has dissolved and bring up to the boil. Pour the hot syrup over the mint leaves and blend until the mint is very finely chopped. Leave the mixture until quite cold and then strain through a muslin-lined sieve into a bowl. Add the lemon juice and then stir in the double cream. Whisk lightly and add a few drops of green food colouring if you like. Turn into a polythene box, put the lid on and freeze until the mixture becomes icy round the edges. Use a fork to turn the sides to the centre and return to the freezer. When the mixture is half frozen turn it into a chilled basin and mix it very thoroughly. Refreeze until firm. Give it half an hour in the fridge to soften a little before serving. This is delicious on its own, or you could accompany it with the orange salad above. Serves 4.

MINT JULEP

This recipe is lovely on a hot day. It comes from *Rosemary Hemphill's Herb Collection*, published by the Aurum Press.

1 large bunch of mint
125g sugar
1 litre pineapple juice
Juice of 4 lemons
3 bottles of dry ginger ale

Wash the mint and put it in a large bowl. Bruise it with a pestle or the end of a rolling pin. Add the sugar and juices and leave to stand in a cool place for two or three hours. Strain into a jug, and when ready to serve add the ginger ale, well chilled, some ice, slices of lemon and sprigs of mint.

CRYSTALLISED MINT LEAVES

Mint leaves
Caster sugar
1 egg white

Pick over the mint leaves, removing any broken or misshapen ones. Break up the egg white with a fork, and then use a small brush to paint both sides of each leaf with the egg white. Put a goodly amount of sugar in a shallow dish and coat each leaf carefully in it. Place the leaves as you finish them on a clean sheet of paper and leave them to dry slowly in a warm and preferably dark place. These will be of a more pastel green than the fresh leaves, but can be useful as a garnish as they hold their shape while fresh mint has an unfortunate tendency to wilt unattractively almost instantly.

MUSHROOM
Agaricus campestris, Boletus edulis etc

From time to time various sorts of wild mushrooms appear in Dr Neil's Garden. Their distinctive flavours are well worth seeking out, but of course you should not eat mushrooms culled from the wild unless you are absolutely certain that they are safe. Occasionally you can find fresh ceps or chanterelles for sale, although in this country at least they will be expensive. Dried ceps (porcini), morels etc are worth using and can be added to ordinary mushrooms. Of the fresh commercial varieties, flat, portabellas or chestnut mushrooms are to be preferred.

WILD MUSHROOM SOUP
This is a recipe of Lesley Waters' in *New to Cooking*, published by Ryland Peters & Small.

   10g dried porcini mushrooms
   50g butter
   500g large flat mushrooms, sliced
   500ml good stock
   2 garlic cloves, crushed
   50g white bread, crusts removed
   150ml sour cream
   Salt and freshly ground black pepper
   Chopped parsley and/or chives

Put the dried porcini in a small bowl, cover with 250ml boiling water, and set aside for 20 minutes or so. Melt the butter in a heavy saucepan and add the fresh mushrooms. Cook over a low heat until soft. Drain the porcini, saving the soaking liquid. Coarsely chop, add to the mushrooms in the pan and cook for a further 2 minutes. Then add the garlic, the bread, torn up, the stock and the reserved mushroom water - carefully, so that you leave behind any fine grit that may be in the bottom of the bowl. Season, bring to the boil and simmer for 10 more minutes. Take off the heat and purée the mixture in a food processor or using a hand-held blender. Reheat briefly if necessary, and serve in bowls with a swirl of crème fraîche and a scatter of parsley or chives. Grind some pepper over all. Serves 4.

STUFFED MUSHROOMS

4 large field or Portabella mushrooms
1 clove garlic, chopped finely
4 olives, black or green, chopped
Cup white breadcrumbs
Salt, pepper and mixed herbs
Butter and olive oil

Wipe the mushrooms clean and remove the stalks. Rub some butter over the skins and place the mushrooms side by side on an oven tray, skin side down. Chop the stalks and add them with the garlic to a knob of butter melted with some oil in a small frying pan. Cook for a minute or two without allowing the garlic to brown and then add the breadcrumbs. Keep the mixture moving in the pan and cook until the crumbs are just beginning to crisp. Take off the heat and stir in the olives, salt, pepper and a sprinkling of fresh or dried herbs to taste. Carefully spoon the crumby mixture on top of the mushrooms - you may need to pat the crumbs down if the mushrooms are very flat, or rise in the middle. Dot the tops with some tiny bits of butter and give them 10 minutes in the oven at 180°C, 375°F, Gas 5. Serves 4 as a starter.

MUSHROOM RISOTTO

250g fresh mushrooms, sliced
10-25g dried porcini mushrooms (ceps)
200g risotto rice
1 small onion, chopped
1 clove garlic, crushed (optional)
1 glass dry white wine
600ml chicken stock
2 tablespoons cream (optional)
Chopped herbs (optional)
Parmesan cheese, grated

If using dried mushrooms, put them in a bowl, cover with hot water and leave to soak for 15 minutes. Put the stock to warm. Soften the onion in a tablespoon of olive oil. Add a knob of butter to the pan and sauté the mushrooms, fresh and reconstituted. Now add the rice, with the garlic and herbs, if using, and stir it all well. Add the wine and when it has been absorbed, start adding the warm stock, a ladleful at a time. Stir frequently and add more stock as needful. When the rice is tender but still retaining some bite, remove from the heat. Adjust the seasoning if necessary, and stir in the cream and 2 or 3 tablespoons of Parmesan. The risotto should be quite moist and you may wish to serve it in bowls rather than on plates. Hand a bowl of more Parmesan with it. Serves 4.

WILD MUSHROOM RAGOÛT
This recipe comes from *The Wildfoods Cookbook* by Joy Spoczynska.

450g ceps (or 400g flat mushrooms + 25g porcini, soaked)
3 medium onions, chopped coarsely
4 medium carrots, sliced
3 tomatoes, skinned and chopped

2 cloves garlic
2 tablespoons chopped parsley
1 heaped tablespoon flour
Salt, black pepper and a pinch of paprika
600ml vegetable stock or water

Put the stock to warm. In a large saucepan soften the onions in a little oil. Add the carrots for another few minutes, without browning and then sprinkle with the flour. Stir round so that any oil is absorbed by the flour and then slowly add the warmed stock or water. Put in the mushrooms, chopped roughly, along with the garlic and seasonings. Bring to the boil and then reduce heat to a simmer and cook until the vegetables are tender but not mushy. Now add the tomatoes, and finally stir in the parsley. This makes a hearty meal, served with pasta or mashed potato. Serves 4.

LITTLE MUSHROOM PIES

250g plain flour
125g butter
Pinch of salt
2 eggs
250g mushrooms, chopped
10g dried porcini mushrooms, soaked in hot water
40g butter
25g grated fresh Parmesan cheese
1 teaspoon chopped herbs
15g walnuts, chopped

To make the pastry, use a processor or rub the 125g butter by hand into the flour with the salt, and then work in one of the eggs and, if needed, a little chilled water to make a dough. Wrap the pastry and leave in the fridge while you make the filling. Drain the porcini mushrooms and chop them. Cook all the mushrooms gently in the 40g butter until all the liquid they release has evaporated. Cool a little, stir in the cheese, nuts and herbs and season the mixture to taste. Beat the second egg lightly and add to the mixture. Roll out the pastry and, using cutters, make circles sufficient to line the wells of a bun tray. Cut slightly smaller circles for the lids. Spoon the mushroom mixture when cold into the bases, moisten the rims with water, and press on the lids. Pierce the top of each little pie, brush with beaten egg or a little milk and bake in a preheated oven at 200°C, 400°F, Gas 6 for 20 minutes. Then turn the heat down to 180°C, 350°F, Gas 4 for a further 20 to 25 minutes. Remove from the oven, carefully ease out the little pies and cool on a wire rack. Makes about 12. These pies make good picnic fare.

NASTURTIUM
Tropaeolum majus

All parts of the nasturtium can be eaten - flower, leaf and seed pod. Flowers and leaves can be eaten just as they are, in salads. An unusual potato salad can be made by adding some leaf, shredded, and a handful of petals. The whole flowers can be used as a handsome garnish for many dishes.

NASTURTIUM POTATO CAKES
This recipe is based on one by Martijn Kajuiter of the Restaurant De Kas in Amsterdam. It was recommended by Jill Dupleix in her column in *The Times*.

> 500g waxy potatoes, peeled
> 2 tablespoons olive oil
> 2 teaspoons finely chopped chives
> 2 teaspoons finely chopped shallots
> Zest of 1 lemon, finely grated
> 1 small garlic clove, crushed
> 60g grated Parmesan cheese
> 2 tablespoons of chopped nasturtium leaves
> Salt and pepper
> 8 slices pancetta or 4 slices streaky bacon to serve

Cook the potatoes in salted water until tender. Drain and mash them, then add the olive oil, chives, shallots, lemon zest, garlic, cheese and nasturtium leaves. Season to taste. Allow the mixture to cool and then shape into cakes - either 4 large ones or 8 smaller ones. Fry them in a little olive oil until golden and crisped on the outside. Grill the pancetta or bacon until crisp and crumble some on top of each cake. Serve with a little green salad garnished with whole nasturtiums. This makes a lovely starter or lunch dish. Alternatively, without the bacon, they are good with fish. Serves 4.

KING'S OWN SAUCE
May Byron included this in her collection of recipes, *Pot Luck*.

Nasturtium flowers
15g shallot, quartered
1 litre white vinegar
15g salt
1 teaspoon cayenne pepper
125ml soy sauce

Pick over the flowers first to remove any small insects and then use them to fill a 1 litre jar or wide necked bottle. Add the shallot and pour in vinegar to the brim. Put on a screwtop lid or other tight cover, and leave in a dark place for 2 months. At the end of that time, strain off the liquor and stir in the salt, cayenne and soy sauce. Decant into small bottles and use as you would Worcestershire Sauce.

PICKLED NASTURTIUM SEEDS or "CAPERS"

Nasturtium seed pods
300ml white vinegar
½ level teaspoon salt
1 bay leaf
3 or 4 peppercorns

Pick the seed pods on a dry day, and then wash and dry them on kitchen paper. Spread them out on a tray and put them in a cool oven for half an hour or so to dry off any remaining water completely. Put the vinegar and other ingredients into a non-aluminium pan, bring to the boil, remove from the heat and infuse for at least 30 minutes, until cool. Pack the seed pods into a jar or jars, and cover with the cold spiced vinegar. Seal in the usual way and keep for 1-2 months before using.

These nasturtium "capers" have a good flavour very similar to true capers, but the texture is firmer. They can be used to replace true capers in recipes such as the two following.

CAPER SAUCE

30g butter
30g flour
300-400ml good stock
2 tablespoons capers
1 tablespoon vinegar from caper jar

Melt the butter and with a wooden spoon work the flour into it gradually. Stir the mixture over gentle heat for a minute or two. Heat the stock and add it gradually to the pan, stirring all the time. Cook for a few minutes and stir in the capers and vinegar immediately before serving. Check the seasoning.

Caper Sauce is a classic accompaniment to roast mutton or lamb and if used in this way juices from the meat can be added to the sauce.

TOMATO AND CAPER SAUCE

2 tomatoes
1 tablespoon capers, rinsed
2 tablespoons olive oil
Finely chopped parsley

With a sharp knife, cut a cross on the base of each tomato. Place them in a small bowl and cover them with freshly boiled water. After a minute or two, pour off the water and peel the skin from the tomatoes. Cut the tomatoes into quarters and, over a sieve placed over a bowl, squeeze out the seeds and juice. Then chop the flesh into small dice. Put the tomato flesh, capers and olive oil into a small pan and gently heat (but do not fry) for 1 minute. Thin if you think it needs it with the reserved tomato juice. Add seasoning and parsley to taste. This is excellent, and looks pretty, served with poached white fish or salmon fillet. Serves 2-3.

PARSLEY
Petroselinum crispum

If you have a large quantity of parsley to chop finely, the easy way to do it without a special gadget is to put the parsley into a small bowl and snip into it repeatedly with scissors.

PARSLEY SOUP
This excellent soup appears in *A Celebration of Soup* by Lindsey Bareham, published by Penguin.

120g butter
3 large leeks, white part only, sliced
3 big bunches of parsley
2 medium potatoes, peeled and chopped
1¼ litres chicken stock
Salt and pepper
142ml cream

Melt the butter in a heavy based pan and cook the leeks and the chopped up parsley stalks gently until soft. Add the potatoes, stock and seasoning and simmer for 20 minutes. Put a handful of parsley leaves on one side and roughly chop the rest. Add to the soup and simmer for 2 minutes. Liquidise the soup to obtain a purée and return to the pan. Add the cream and the remainder of the parsley chopped very fine, heat through and adjust the seasoning. Serves 6.

PARSLEY CREAM SAUCE
You can make a parsley sauce of course by stirring chopped parsley into an ordinary béchamel or white sauce but for something special - asparagus, say, or for fillets of white fish or salmon, this more delicate sauce is delicious. Jane Grigson recommends it in her Vegetable Book.

125g butter
142ml whipping or double cream
Salt, pepper and lemon juice
2-3 tablespoons chopped parsley

Melt the butter gently in a frying pan. When it starts to bubble, stir in the cream thoroughly until it has amalgamated smoothly with the butter. Away from the heat, add salt, pepper and a squeeze of lemon juice. Stir in the parsley and return to a gentle heat briefly to warm through again. It must not boil. Serve immediately.

MAÎTRE D'HÔTEL BUTTER

60g butter
1 tablespoon parsley, finely chopped
1 teaspoon lemon juice
Salt and pepper

Beat the butter to a creamy softness. Stir in the parsley and the lemon juice. Add a little salt and pepper to taste. Chill and serve in pats on hot food - steaks, cod or haddock, or vegetables.

WELSH PARSLEY PANCAKES

250g flour
3-4 tablespoons chopped parsley
1 tablespoon chopped chives
2 beaten eggs
Milk
Salt and pepper

Make a mixture by making a well in the flour and working the eggs and milk in gradually and then beating thoroughly until smooth. This can be done easily in a food processor. Season and add the parsley. Leave to stand for half an hour. The batter should be of a creamy pouring consistency. If it seems too thick, add some more milk. Fry the pancakes in a hot frying pan with just enough butter or oil to stop them sticking. Eat them on their own, warm with butter, or serve them with bacon or with sausages.

PARSLEY QUICHE

This is a recipe of Jane Grigson's which she gives in her book *Good Things*. The cheese is an addition.

    125g flour
    60g butter
    1 teaspoon icing sugar
    1 egg, beaten
    250g onion, chopped
    1 clove garlic, finely chopped (optional)
    90g butter
    280ml cream
    2 eggs, beaten
    1 tablespoon grated Gruyère or Cheddar cheese
    4 tablespoons parsley, finely chopped
    1 tablespoon chopped chives

Stir the sugar into the flour and then rub in the butter. Work in the egg until the mixture coheres. Roll it out on a floured board and use it to line a flan ring (c.23cm diameter). For the filling, melt the butter in a saucepan and add the chopped onion and garlic. Cook gently until the onion is transparent and pale gold in colour. Leave to cool a little while you beat the cream and eggs together and then stir in the cheese, the parsley, chives and seasoning. Spread the cooked onion over the base of the flan case and then pour the parsley mixture over the top. Cook in a moderate oven, 190°C, 375°F, Gas 5, for 40 minutes, turning the temperature down towards the end of the cooking time if the quiche is browning too much. This cooks to an exciting green colour and looks - and tastes - good served with a tomato salad. Serves 4-6.

PHEASANT
Phasianus colchicus

Pheasants roost in Dr Neil's Garden, and from time to time the cocks are to be seen strolling about in their exotic plumage, accompanied on occasion by their much less gorgeously equipped mates.

PHEASANT BREASTS PIMENTO
This is adapted from a recipe of Lilli Gore's in *Game Cooking*.

> 4 pheasant breasts
> 80g streaky bacon, or pancetta, chopped
> 1 onion, sliced
> 1 carrot, diced
> Olive oil
> 1 clove garlic
> Bouquet garni
> Stock
> 1 sweet red pepper
> 125g chorizo sausage, cut in chunks
> Salt and pepper

Put the oil into a heavy pan and brown the onion, carrot and bacon lightly. Remove the vegetables and brown the pheasant breasts, adding more oil if you need it. Return the vegetables and bacon to the pan and add the bouquet garni, garlic and enough stock to cover. Bring to a simmer, cover the pan and cook very gently for 20 minutes. Add the red pepper and the sausage to the pan, and continue to cook for another 5-10 minutes until the meat is tender. Remove the pheasant breasts and keep warm while continuing to cook the vegetables with the sausage until soft but not mushy. Thicken the sauce if you like with a little slaked cornflour, and adjust seasoning. Sprinkle with a goodly amount of chopped parsley (this looks brilliant) and serve with boiled rice. Serves 4.

PHEASANT WITH CHESTNUTS IN RED WINE

Annette Hope gives this recipe in *A Caledonian Feast*. She recommends it for a dinner party, as it is easy, glamorous, and ensures that the pheasant will be moist and delicious.

1 brace pheasants
40g butter
2 tablespoons olive oil
250g dried chestnuts, soaked for at least 24 hours
375g button onions
2 tablespoons flour
450ml chicken stock
Grated rind and juice of 1orange
1 tablespoon redcurrant jelly
2 good glasses red wine
Bouquet garni, with lovage or a stick of celery
Salt and pepper

Heat the oil and butter gently in a large frying pan and brown the birds slowly. Then transfer them to a large casserole. Put the onions and chestnuts into the frying pan and cook briskly for a few minutes, shaking the pan, until they change colour. Using a slotted spoon add them to the birds. Add the flour to the butter mixture remaining, stir well and cook for 2-3 minutes. Then gradually pour in the stock, orange juice with the rind, the jelly and the wine, stirring constantly until smooth. Add salt and pepper and pour over the birds. Cover and put in a moderate oven, 170°-180°C, 325°-350°F, Gas 3-4, for 1½-2 hours.

Turn off the heat 10 minutes before serving. Dish the birds on a large ashet with the onions and chestnuts. Keep warm while you boil the liquid rapidly, reducing it by a third. Pour a little over the birds, and hand the remainder separately. Serves 7-8.

PHEASANT WITH CREAM AND APPLES

This recipe sounds a little rich, but if the pheasant meat is at all dry - and it often is - the cream comes as a welcome addition to the sauce. It comes from *The New Times Cook Book* by Shona Crawford Poole.

2 young pheasants, trussed with fat bacon for roasting
Salt and freshly ground black pepper
85g butter
2 shallots, peeled
450g Cox's orange pippin apples
6 tablespoons game stock or water
4 tablespoons Calvados or brandy
142ml double cream

Put a knob of butter rolled in salt and pepper and a peeled shallot inside each bird and place them in a roasting tin. Roast in a preheated oven 220°C, 425F, Gas 7, for about 45 minutes until cooked to your liking. Tip the juices from inside the birds into the roasting tin and put the birds to rest in a warm place until you are ready to carve them.

While the pheasants are roasting, peel, core and thickly slice the apples. Melt the remaining butter in a frying pan and sauté the apples until they are softened and beginning to brown a little. Transfer the apple slices to a serving dish and keep warm. Carve the pheasants and arrange the meat on the apples. Cover and continue to keep warm while you make the sauce. Skim any fat from the roasting tin and stir in the stock or water. Cook over a high heat, scraping up the crusty bits until the liquid has reduced by half. Strain this liquid into a small saucepan, add the alcohol, heat for a minute or so, and then add the cream. Reduce until the sauce has thickened slightly, adjust the seasoning, and pour over the pheasant and apples. Serve with a simple salad garnish and tiny potatoes. Serves 4.

PIGEON
Columba palumbus

PIGEON IN A PASTRY
This recipe is based on one of Geraldene Holt's in *French Country Kitchen*.

    4 medium-sized croissants
    4 pigeon breasts, sliced thinly
    2 slices of streaky bacon, or 4 of pancetta, chopped
    1 shallot, finely chopped
    250ml red wine
    250ml stock, chicken, or made from pigeon carcases
    125g oyster or other mushrooms, finely sliced
    45g butter
    Salt and ground black pepper

First slice the croissants horizontally not quite across so that they are hinged and place on a baking sheet ready for the oven. They will need about 5 minutes at 180°C, 350°F, Gas 4 just before serving. Heat 30g of the butter and cook the bacon and shallot until just starting to colour. Add the slices of meat and sauté for 2-3 minutes. Lastly add the mushrooms and when they are cooked remove all the meat and vegetables to a covered dish and keep warm.
Pour the wine and stock into the pan and bring to the boil, stirring to scrape up any tasty morsels left on the pan. Reduce to about half the quantity, and if it seems too thin you could thicken it with a little slaked cornflour. Add the remaining butter, and pour over the meat and vegetables. To serve, put one crisped croissant on each plate, open the 'lids' and divide the pigeon and mushroom mixture between them. Serves 4 as a starter.

PIGEON AND GUINNESS CASSEROLE

This really good recipe comes from *The Poacher's Cookbook* by Prue Coats, published by Merlin Unwin Books.

16-20 pigeon breasts, cut into chunks
125g streaky bacon
50g butter or oil
10 shallots, peeled and left whole
4 carrots, cut into rounds
50g flour
300ml Guinness or dark ale
150ml stock, preferably made from pigeon carcases
1 tablespoon dark muscovado sugar
2 teaspoons concentrated tomato purée
Salt, pepper and red wine vinegar
1 teaspoon redcurrant jelly (optional)

Brown the pigeon breasts and the bacon in the butter or oil, and then add the vegetables and cook for a few minutes. Sprinkle in the flour and stir to absorb. Add the Guinness, stock, sugar, tomato purée and seasoning, and transfer to a casserole. Cook with the lid on at 200°C, 400°F, Gas 6 for 15 minutes, and then at 160°C, 325°F, Gas 3 for 2-3 hours. Check that it does not start to dry out. Just before serving, add a dash of vinegar, and the jelly if you think it is needed. Serves 6-8.

PIGEON CASSEROLE PROVENÇALE

This recipe comes from *Game Cooking* by Lilli Gore.

4 pigeons
125g bacon, diced
90g butter
2 glasses wine, red or white
600ml stock
1 clove garlic, chopped

12 black olives, stoned
12 button onions
3 tomatoes, skinned and roughly chopped
Bouquet garni, salt and pepper
8 anchovy fillets (optional)
1 tablespoon chopped parsley

Using a heavy pan, brown the birds and the bacon in 60g of the butter. Add the wine, stock, garlic, tomatoes, bouquet garni, salt and pepper. Add the anchovies, cut in three, if you are using them, but in this case omit the salt. Put on the lid and place in the oven at 160°C, 325°F, Gas 3 for 2-3 hours. Half an hour before serving, sauté the onions in the remaining butter and add to the casserole along with the olives. Serve sprinkled with the parsley. Serves 4.

PIGEON BREASTS WITH CELERY AND WALNUTS
Claire Macdonald (www.claire-macdonald.com) includes this recipe in her admirable *More Seasonal Cooking*.

12 pigeon breasts
5 tablespoons olive oil
2 onions, skinned and sliced
7 sticks celery, thinly sliced
300ml red wine
6 juniper berries, crushed
A few sprigs parsley, roughly chopped
2 cloves garlic, chopped
1 tablespoon flour
150ml stock, preferably made with pigeon carcases
1 tablespoon crab apple or redcurrant jelly
Salt and pepper
50g butter
75g shelled walnuts

Heat 3 tablespoons of the oil in a pan and add the onion and one of the sliced stalks of celery. Cook for 5 minutes without browning, then pour in the wine and add the juniper berries, parsley and garlic. Simmer for 5 minutes and then leave to cool completely. When the marinade is cold, pour it over the pigeon breasts in a shallow bowl and leave to marinate for several hours (or overnight), turning the meat from time to time. When you are ready to cook, fish out the pigeon breasts and dry them on paper towels. Heat the remaining oil in a frying pan and cook the breasts for about 2 minutes on each side if you like them pink inside, or for a little longer if not. Remove from the pan and keep them warm.

Sprinkle the flour into the pan to absorb any oil and then add the strained marinade, the stock and the jelly. Heat gently until the jelly has melted (commercial jelly can be slow to melt) and then bring the sauce to the boil. Taste and adjust the seasoning. To make the garnish melt the butter in a small frying pan and put in the remaining celery and the walnuts. Keep them moving as you cook them for 10 minutes. To serve, slice the pigeon breasts in half horizontally and place 4 halves on a pool of sauce on each plate. Divide the celery and walnut mixture over the top. Serves 6.

RABBIT
Oryctolagus cuniculus

Rabbit as a foodstuff has rather fallen from favour, but it is worth re-discovering. The mild, white meat can be delicious.

RABBIT WITH MUSTARD
Margaret Costa gave this recipe in her *Four Seasons Cookery*.

    4 joints of rabbit
    4 tablespoons French mustard, preferably tarragon-flavoured
    1 rounded tablespoon seasoned flour
    45g butter
    60g mild bacon, diced
    1 onion, finely chopped
    1 clove garlic, crushed
    280ml single cream
    Salt and pepper

The day before you want to eat the rabbit, put the joints to soak in cold salted water. After a couple of hours, drain them and dry them on kitchen paper. Then coat them all over with the mustard and leave in a cool place. Next day sift the flour over the joints and then brown them lightly in the butter. Remove from the pan and put them in a heatproof casserole. In the pan cook the diced bacon for a few minutes, and then add the onion and the garlic and cook until they are soft but not coloured. Add the contents of the pan to the rabbit, and with the lid on the casserole cook over a low heat for 30 minutes. Pour in the cream and place the casserole this time in the oven 160°C, 325°F, Gas 3 for about 45 minutes. Stir it once or twice in this time, and finally add some salt and pepper to taste. To serve, sprinkle with some finely chopped parsley and, if you like, accompany it with some small triangles of bread fried crisp in butter. Serves 4.

RABBIT IN CIDER
This useful recipe is from *Plats du Jour* by Patience Gray and
Primrose Boyd.

    1 rabbit, in 4 pieces
    2 tablespoons olive oil
    Juice of half a lemon
    2 medium onions, sliced
    60g lean bacon or ham, chopped
    1 tablespoon flour
    250g tomatoes, peeled and roughly chopped (or use
        canned)
    Salt and pepper
    1 bay leaf and some thyme
    150ml dry cider

Put the pieces of rabbit to soak for an hour in cold water with
the lemon juice added. Then remove the rabbit and dry it well
on kitchen paper. Heat the oil and brown the meat in it, then
remove and keep warm. Soften the onions over gentle heat and
then add the bacon. Sprinkle the flour over the contents of the
pan, stir and add the tomatoes and then the cider. Return the
rabbit to the pan and add the herbs and seasoning. Cover the
pan closely and cook on a low heat for approximately 1¼
hours, checking from time to time that there is still sufficient
liquid. Taste, remove the bay leaf, and adjust the seasoning if
necessary before serving with mashed potato. Serves 3-4.

SPANISH STYLE RABBIT
Lilli Gore gives this recipe in her *Game Cooking*.

    1 rabbit, in 4 pieces
    60g bacon or chorizo sausage, chopped
    2 tablespoons olive oil
    2 cloves garlic, chopped
    1 bay leaf

1 clove
1 tablespoon chopped parsley
1 glass white wine
10g dark chocolate

Put the oil in a heavy pan and first fry the bacon if you are
using it. Remove the bacon while you brown the rabbit pieces.
Return the bacon and add the garlic, bay leaf, parsley, clove,
the chorizo if you are using that, the white wine and the
chocolate. Stir everything round so that the rabbit is covered
equally with the mixture. Season with salt and pepper and add
a cup of water. Cover with a lid and simmer for 1¼ hours.
Serve with boiled rice. Serves 3-4.

RHUBARB
Rheum ponticum

The rhubarb in Dr Neil's Garden came originally from the garden at Prestonfield House, on the other side of the Loch. Thus we believe it to be descended from the rhubarb which in 1774 won for Sir Alexander Dick of Prestonfield a gold medal from the Society for the Encouragement of Arts, Manufactures and Commerce for the best British specimen. Sir Alexander, who had qualified as a doctor of medicine, also presented some seeds of his rhubarb to Dr Johnson, of Dictionary renown.

SPRING RHUBARB SOUP
This is slightly adapted from Ruth Lowinsky's recipe in her book *More Lovely Food*.

450g young rhubarb
2 onions, sliced
1 carrot, chopped
30g uncooked ham, chopped
60g butter
2 litres chicken stock
90g fresh white breadcrumbs
Salt, cayenne pepper, sugar

Peel the rhubarb and cut into large pieces. Blanch them in boiling water for a few minutes, and then drain them thoroughly. Melt the butter in a large pan and add the rhubarb, onion and ham. Cook gently without browning until the rhubarb is soft. Add the stock and breadcrumbs and simmer for 15 minutes. Season with salt, pepper and, cautiously, with sugar. The soup should not be sweet, but some sugar may be necessary to neutralise the tartness. Liquidise or put through a food processor. Reheat, and dilute further if it is too thick. Serve with croûtons fried in butter. Serves 8.

RHUBARB AND GOATS' CHEESE TART

    125g plain flour
    60g butter
    1 teaspoon icing sugar
    1 egg, beaten
    450g rhubarb, chopped
    20g sugar
    2 small goats' cheeses, 60g each
    8 walnut halves, roughly chopped
    Freshly ground black pepper

Rub the butter into the flour and icing sugar and then work in the beaten egg. Roll it out and use to line a 22cm flan tin, preferably with a removable base. Inside the pastry fit some baking paper and weight it down with baking beans. Bake the pastry shell for 10-15 minutes at 190°C, 375°F, Gas 5. Take it out of the oven, remove the paper and beans and return to the oven for another 5 minutes to crisp the base. Cook the rhubarb gently with just a tiny splash of water to preserve its shape. Pare the rind from the top and bottom of the cheeses and slice them into medallions about 5mm thick. Drain the rhubarb well, taste it and sprinkle a little sugar over it if necessary. It should not be obviously sweet, but neither should it be fiercely tart. Spoon the rhubarb into the pastry shell, distribute the goats' cheese over the top and sprinkle over the chopped walnuts. Return to the oven for 10-15 minutes to partly melt the cheese and to heat through. Divide into 6 segments and serve with some freshly ground black pepper and a salad garnish. Serves 6 as a starter.

RHUBARB FOOL
This recipe and the next one come from Margaret Costa's *Four Seasons Cookery*.

450g rhubarb, chopped
60-90g demerara sugar
Rind of 1 small orange, finely grated
142-200ml thick cream
2 teaspoons Pernod (optional)

Put the rhubarb, sugar and orange rind in a covered dish and cook in a slow oven until it is soft. Do not cook it too long as it will lose colour. Drain the rhubarb and put it in a blender, or sieve it. When it is quite cold, stir in the cream. If you are using very rich cream - Jersey, for instance - the smaller quantity will probably be sufficient. If the cream is more liquid, you may need more of it and it may be best to whip it a little first. Stir in the Pernod if you are using it - its aniseed flavour complements the rhubarb very well. Divide the mixture into 4 glass dishes and then leave the fools to stand in a cool place for an hour or so. Serve with thin shortbread biscuits. Serves 4.

RHUBARB WITH SOUR CREAM

450g rhubarb, prepared and cooked as in the last recipe
142ml soured cream, or crème fraîche
Demerara sugar

Cook the rhubarb as above, taking care that the pieces keep their shape. As soon as it is cool enough, use a slotted spoon to divide the rhubarb into individual glasses. Chill and then top each glass with soured cream - or you could use yoghurt if you prefer. Sprinkle each one with demerara sugar to make a crunchy topping and serve straight away. Serves 4.

RHUBARB SOUFFLÉ

This recipe has been slightly adapted from Jill Dupleix's original, given in her column in *The Times*.

200g rhubarb, chopped
2 tablespoons caster sugar
3 eggs, separated, plus 2 extra egg whites
100g caster sugar
40g candied orange peel, finely chopped
Icing sugar

Cook the rhubarb with the 2 tablespoons of sugar and a dash of water until soft. Prepare individual soufflé dishes by smearing with softened butter and dusting with caster sugar. Preheat the oven to 190°C, 375°F, Gas 5. Beat the three egg yolks in a bowl with 60g of the sugar until it is pale and thick. Add the cooked rhubarb, leaving behind any excess of liquid, and beat well. Whisk the five egg whites and 20g of the sugar in a clean bowl until the whites start to thicken. Add the remaining sugar and keep whisking until soft peaks form. Gently fold the egg whites into the yolk mixture, one third at a time. Fold in the orange peel and then spoon the soufflé mix into the prepared dishes, filling them to the top. Bake for 12 to 15 minutes until puffed and coloured. Dust with icing sugar and serve immediately. Serves 4-6.

RHUBARB AND GRAPEFRUIT JAM

This excellent recipe comes from Pamela Westland's *A Taste of the Country*.

750g trimmed, washed rhubarb
2 grapefruit
750g sugar

Put the rhubarb into a bowl, or straight into the preserving pan, and finely grate the grapefruit rind over it. Place a small chopping board inside a large shallow dish (to catch the juice) and using a sharp knife cut away all the grapefruit rind and pith. Then carefully cut towards the centre of each fruit releasing each segment from its adjoining membrane. Cut each segment into three or four. Add all the fruit and the juice to the rhubarb. Pour the sugar over all and leave overnight. Next day, bring slowly to the boil, stirring often. When the sugar has completely dissolved, raise the heat and boil hard until setting point is reached. Pot in the usual way.

This jam makes an excellent alternative to marmalade, or try it as a relish with roast duck.

ROSE
Rosa damascena, centifolia, gallica etc

Roses should be culled after the morning dew has disappeared and before the heat of mid day. The petals should be picked off gently, removing any insects as you go. The white "heel" of each petal (which is bitter-tasting) should be snipped out, using scissors.

CRAB APPLE AND ROSE PETAL JELLY
This recipe comes from Jekka McVicar's *Cooking with Flowers* published by Kyle Cathie.

> 1¾ kg crab apples, washed and chopped
> Approx 1½ kg sugar
> Petals of 3 large highly scented roses

Put the apples into a capacious pan with enough water to cover them and bring to the boil. Simmer until the fruit becomes really soft. Strain through a jelly bag or a muslin-lined sieve, and leave to drip for several hours or overnight. Measure the juice and return it to the (washed out) pan with 450g sugar to every 600ml juice. Prepare the rose petals by snipping out the white heels and then tie all but 1 tablespoon of them into a muslin bag, loosely packed. Bring the sugared juice to the boil and add the bag of petals. Boil for about 20 minutes until setting point is reached and then remove the muslin bag. Tear into smaller pieces any large petals amongst the reserved ones, and stir them into the jelly. Pour into clean, warmed jars and cover in the usual way.

If, as is quite likely, your most fragrant roses will be over before crab apples are available, you can use ordinary cooking apples instead, with the addition of the juice from 2 lemons.

ROSE PETAL ICE CREAM

This recipe comes from Jenny Leggatt's *Cooking with Flowers.*

275ml single cream
Petals of 1-2 large sweet smelling roses (20-40g)
4 egg yolks
50g caster sugar
284ml double cream, lightly whipped
1-2 teaspoons rose water
Colouring

Prepare the petals by snipping out the white heels and put them with the single cream into a saucepan. Heat gently until the cream is just warm, remove from the heat and leave to infuse for 20 minutes. Then heat it again and as soon as it boils, remove it from the heat and infuse for another 20 minutes. Sieve it to remove the petals.

Whisk together the egg yolks and sugar, then whisk in the rose flavoured cream. Pour the mixture back into the pan and cook over a low heat, stirring continuously, until the custard is thick enough to coat the back of a wooden spoon. Leave to cool.

Beat the double cream until it has increased in volume and is not much stiffer than the custard. Fold the two together with the rose water and a drop or two of food colouring if you like, and turn into an ice tray or plastic box.

Freeze until the edges are firm and then stir it sides to middle. Freeze again until it is firm throughout, but not brick hard. If you have a Kenwood mixer or something similar, you can break it into lumps and then beat it to aerate it further, before returning it to the freezer. If no such heavy-duty mixer is available give the mixture some extra stirring while it is freezing. Either way, move it from the freezer to the fridge about an hour before you want to eat it, to allow it to soften. Serves 6.

CRYSTALLISED ROSE PETALS

Rose petals
Caster sugar
Egg white, lightly beaten

Prepare the petals as above. Use a children's painting brush to coat the petals all over with egg white. Immediately dip each petal in caster sugar and place on a rack in a warm place to dry. The sugar should become hard and dry. You will probably find that the undersides of the petals will reject the egg white, and will remain uncoated. Nevertheless, they will keep quite well for 2-3 days in an airtight container.

ROSE PETAL CAKE
Jekka McVicar gives this recipe in her *Cooking with Flowers*.

175g butter
175g caster sugar
3 tablespoons rose petals
3 medium eggs, separated
175g self-raising flour
1 teaspoon baking powder
2 teaspoons rose water

Prepare two sandwich tins (20-22cm in diameter) by greasing and flouring them. Prepare the rose petals by removing the white heels and tearing any large petals into smaller pieces. Cream the butter and sugar together until light and fluffy. Beat the egg yolks one by one into the mixture and then fold in the rose petals and the flour sieved with the baking powder. Stir in the rose water. Beat the egg whites until they are stiff and fold gently into the mixture. Divide the mixture between the two tins and bake at 180°C, 350F, Gas 4 for approximately 30 minutes. The cakes are done when a skewer pushed into the centre of the cakes comes out clean. Turn the cakes onto a wire tray to cool.

Sandwich the cakes together with some rose petal jelly or make a filling with 75g butter and 100g sieved icing sugar worked together and flavoured with 1-2 tablespoons rose water. An icing for the top may be made with 225g sifted icing sugar and rosewater. Decorate with crystallised rose petals. This makes a lovely cake for a summer birthday.

ROSEHIP SYRUP

    1kg rosehips
    450g sugar

Pick over the hips, removing any which are damaged or not quite red, and any leaves. Wash them and then bring 1½ litres of water to the boil in a capacious pan and add the hips to it. Bring back to the boil and as soon as the hips have softened sufficiently, use a potato masher to break them down in the pan. Continue to cook, adding more water if necessary and stirring frequently to prevent burning, until you have a soft pulpy mass. Cool a little and then strain through a fine muslin or jelly bag. When the dripping has stopped return the pulp to the pan with another litre of boiling water. Cook for a few minutes and then cool again and strain as before. Combine the two extracts and boil again until you have about 900ml. Measure the quantity and stir in 450g sugar to 900ml extract, and then boil the mixture for 5 minutes. Pour while still hot into sterilised bottles or jars, seal and when cold, store in the fridge.

This makes a thick, slightly cloudy syrup which can be used on its own as a sauce, or as the sweetener for stewed fruit. Apple cooked with it makes an unusual accompaniment to roast pork.

ROSEMARY
Rosmarinus officinalis

COURGETTE AND ROSEMARY SOUP
This delicious soup comes from *More Seasonal Cooking* by
Claire Macdonald (www.claire-macdonald.com).

750g courgettes, trimmed and sliced
2 medium onions, chopped
1 garlic clove, chopped
2 teaspoons fresh rosemary leaves
1¼ litres chicken stock
2 tablespoons oil
Salt and black pepper

Warm the oil in a saucepan and add the chopped onions. Cook
them gently without browning for about 5 minutes, stirring
occasionally, and then add the courgettes. Cook for a further 5
minutes and then add the garlic, rosemary, stock, and some salt
and pepper. Simmer for 25 minutes. Allow to cool a little and
then liquidise. Adjust the seasoning. Either reheat to serve hot,
or chill to serve cold. For chilled soup a swirl of yoghurt and
some chopped chives is a good addition. Serves 6-8.

ROSEMARY POTATO GRATIN

750g potatoes
2 teaspoons rosemary leaves, chopped
30g butter
150ml cream
150ml milk
Freshly ground salt and pepper

Butter a shallow oven dish generously. Peel and finely slice the potatoes and immediately put in layers into the dish, sprinkling with the rosemary, salt and pepper as you go. Warm the milk and cream together in a small saucepan and pour the warm mixture over the potatoes. Dot the top with tiny pieces of the remaining butter and bake at 190°C, 375°F, Gas 5 for about an hour. Serves 4.

ROSEMARY CREAM WITH RASPBERRIES

284ml cream
40g caster sugar
6 stalks of fresh rosemary
350g raspberries

Put the cream, sugar and rosemary into a heavy pan. Heat at the lowest setting for 10 minutes, stirring occasionally and pushing the rosemary down into the cream. Make sure the sugar is dissolved before you turn off the heat, and leave to infuse. When cool, strain the cream into a bowl and chill it. Serve the cream spooned over the berries in small dishes. This cream is good too with pears or bananas. Serves 4-6.

ROSEMARY SHORTBREAD

1 tablespoon roughly chopped rosemary
175g butter
75g caster sugar
175g plain flour
75g semolina or rice flour

Whiz the rosemary with the caster sugar in a food processor until it is very finely chopped. Beat the butter until softened and then gradually add the sugar and rosemary mix, and continue to beat until soft and fluffy. Stir in the flour and semolina and work it until it sticks together. Turn out onto a lightly floured board and knead briefly until smooth. Roll it out thinly (about ½ cm thick). Use a cutter to make individual biscuits and place them slightly apart on a baking tray. Gather up the cuttings and re-roll them to make more biscuits. Prick them with a fork and cook in a pre-heated oven at 180°C, 350°F, Gas 4 for 15 minutes until faintly coloured. Spread on a rack, dust with caster sugar and leave to cool.

GOOSEBERRY AND ROSEMARY ICE CREAM

450g gooseberries
125g caster sugar
2 or 3 stalks of rosemary
280ml double cream

Wash the fruit but there is no need to top and tail it. Put it and the sugar in a pan with 3 tablespoons water. Add the rosemary leaves stripped from the stalks. Simmer over a low heat stirring occasionally until the berries are soft but not discoloured. When the fruit mixture is cool, put it through a blender and then through a sieve. Make sure this purée is quite cold before whipping the cream lightly and folding the two together. Turn into a plastic box or other container with a lid and place in the freezer. Stir the ice cream vigorously sides to middle several times during the freezing process. Serves 4-6.

ROWAN
Sorbus ancuparia

ROWAN JELLY

> 2kg rowan berries
> 4 tablespoons lemon juice
> Sugar

Pull the berries off the stems, wash and put in the pan with 1 litre of water and the lemon juice. Bring to the boil and simmer gently for 45-60 minutes to extract the juice. Strain through a jelly bag or a muslin-lined sieve, and leave overnight to drip. Next day measure the liquid and return it to the preserving pan. When it has come to the boil, take it off the heat and add 450g sugar for every 600ml of liquid, and stir until it is dissolved. Then bring again to the boil and boil briskly until setting point is reached (221°F on a sugar thermometer). Pot and cover in the usual way.
This jelly has a faint bitterness to it, and is excellent with venison or other game.

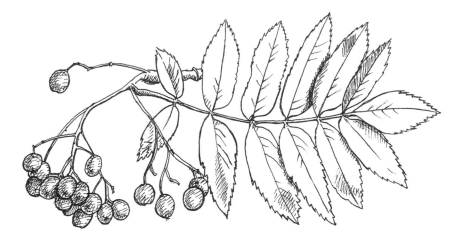

STRAWBERRY
Fragaria vesca

The tiny Alpine strawberries grow in Dr Neil's Garden. These recipes can all be made with ordinary cultivated strawberries, but are particularly good with the tiny ones if you are able to amass enough of them. Or you can use a mixture, making up the weight of the wild berries with cultivated ones.

WILD STRAWBERRY SHORTCAKE
This recipe comes from *The Poacher's Cookbook* by Prue Coats, published by Merlin Unwin Books.

> 175g plain flour
> 125g butter, cut into small pieces
> 75g ground almonds
> 130g caster sugar
> 1 egg, separated
> 250g strawberries
> 150ml crème fraîche

Sift the flour with a pinch of salt, add the butter and whiz in a processor for 15 seconds. Add the almonds, 80g of the caster sugar and the egg yolk, and process again until the mixture coheres. Divide into two and roll out to make two circles 15cm in diameter. Score one lightly into 6 or 8 segments. Place them on a greased baking sheet, prick with a fork and cook at 160°C, 325°F, Gas 3 for 30 minutes. Cool slightly and transfer to a wire tray. If using cultivated strawberries, hull them and if necessary cut into smaller pieces. Sprinkle the berries with half the remaining sugar. Whisk the egg white until stiff, add the last of the sugar and continue beating until it is thick. Beat the crème fraîche and fold it into the egg white. Fold in the strawberries. Sandwich the pastry rounds with this mixture, sprinkle with icing sugar and serve immediately. Serves 6-8.

STRAWBERRIES WITH MARSALA

Strawberries, preferably tiny ones
Caster sugar
Marsala

Put prepared berries in a bowl, sprinkle with caster sugar and then pour over them a glass or so of Marsala. Leave to macerate for about 30 minutes, turning the berries gently once. This is lovely with ice cream.

STRAWBERRY TARTLETS

125g butter, softened
2 tablespoons vanilla sugar
1 large egg, beaten
Pinch salt
250g flour
Redcurrant jelly
Strawberries
125g mascarpone or other cream cheese

Cream the butter and sugar, then add the egg and salt. When fairly well amalgamated, work in the flour. Chill the dough in the fridge for at least 30 minutes. Then roll it out thinly and line some tartlet tins. Prick with a fork and cook at 200°C, 400°F, Gas 6 for 10 minutes, and then at 180°C, 350°F, Gas 4 until lightly browned. Slowly melt 2 tablespoons of redcurrant jelly with 1 tablespoon of water. When your tartlets are cool, use a pastry brush to paint them inside with some of this glaze. Soften the cheese by working with a fork, and add a little cream if you like. Spoon some softened cheese into each tartlet and arrange strawberries on the top. Finally add some more glaze over the fruit. (This may be easier with a spoon rather than the brush.)

STRAWBERRY ICE CREAM

Elizabeth David recommends this recipe for wild strawberries. She gives it in *Summer Cooking*.

900g strawberries
250g sugar
Juice of half a lemon
Juice of half an orange
142ml double cream

Sieve the strawberries to produce 600ml strawberry juice. (This is easier if you put the berries through a blender first.) Make a syrup with the sugar and 150ml water by boiling together for 5 minutes. When the syrup is cold add it to the strawberry pulp and add the lemon and orange juice. Whip the cream until it has thickened and increased in volume but is not stiff. Stir the strawberry pulp gently into the cream, adding the fruit a little at a time. Turn the mixture into a container with a lid and freeze. Stir several times during the freezing. Serves 6 or 7.

STRAWBERRY FOOL

450g strawberries
90g caster sugar
142ml double cream

If you wash the berries, make sure you dry them carefully. Hull cultivated berries (after washing) and mash and then sieve all the berries. Tip in the sugar and stir until all the sugar is dissolved. Whip the cream until it is holding its shape, and, a spoonful at a time, stir the fruit purée into it. Chill and serve in individual glass bowls. Serves 4.

TANSY
Tanacetum vulgare

When chopping tansy, first cut out and discard the central rib of the leaf. The rest is soft and easily chopped.

CARROT AND TANSY SOUP

>1 onion, chopped
>500g carrots, cleaned and sliced
>1 sprig tansy, stripped from its stem
>1 litre stock
>Salt, pepper and nutmeg

Soften onion for a few minutes in a little oil. Add the carrots, tansy and stock, and cook gently until carrots are soft. Cool slightly and then liquidise. Stir in a couple of pinches of nutmeg and adjust the seasoning if necessary. Serves 4.

TANSY CAKES

>125g plain flour
>125g butter
>125g caster sugar
>½ level teaspoon baking powder
>2 teaspoons chopped tansy leaves
>2 eggs, beaten

Sift the flour with the baking powder. Cream the butter and sugar. Add some of the flour to this mix, and then some of the egg. Go on adding alternately until it is all amalgamated and then stir in the chopped tansy. Grease the wells of a bun tray and drop a tablespoon of dough into each. Bake at 190°C, 375°F, Gas 5 for 12-15 minutes. Cool on a wire tray.

CHEESE SAVOURIES WITH TANSY

80g plain flour
Salt and cayenne pepper
80g butter
80g grated Cheddar
2 heaped teaspoons of finely chopped tansy
Beaten egg to glaze

Sift the flour with a little salt and a small pinch of cayenne into a bowl. Chop the butter into small pieces and then rub it into the flour, or process it. Add the cheese and tansy and work it together to make a dough. Roll out thinly and brush all over with the beaten egg. Cut into 5cm wide strips, then across into squares and then diagonally into triangles. Spread out on a baking sheet and bake at 190°C, 375°F, Gas 5 for about 10 minutes until golden. Remove to a wire tray to cool and crisp.

TANSY SCONES

350g self-raising flour
½ teaspoon salt
A little extra baking powder
30g butter
300ml milk
3 rounded teaspoons finely chopped tansy

Sieve the dry ingredients into a bowl and rub in the butter. Stir in the tansy and enough milk to make a coherent but not sloppy dough. Turn the mixture out on a well-floured surface and work it lightly. Roll or pat it out until it is approximately 2cm thick. With a knife divide the dough into squares, or use a circular cutter. Transfer the scones to a baking tray and bake at 220°C, 425°F, Gas 7 for 10-15 minutes until risen and golden brown. Delicious served warm with butter or apple jelly.

THYME
Thymus vulgaris

CHICKEN WITH LEMON AND THYME

8 good-sized chicken thighs
Grated rind of ½ lemon
2 teaspoons thyme leaves
8 preserved lemons, halved
12 black olives, stoned
Olive oil
A glass of white wine or chicken stock
Salt and black pepper

Preheat the oven to 180°C, 350°F, Gas 4. Dry the chicken thighs if necessary with kitchen paper and brown them in a little oil in a frying pan. Place the chicken pieces side by side in a close-fitting ovenproof dish, tuck in the lemon halves and olives, and sprinkle with olive oil, thyme, salt and black pepper. Pour in the stock or wine, cover with a lid or foil and bake for 40 minutes. Check once or twice during the cooking time to see if you need to top up with some more liquid - it should not cook dry. Serves 4.

TOMATO AND THYME TART

150g flour
75g butter, chilled
2 yolks and 1 white of egg
Chilled water
500g large firm tomatoes
2 tablespoons cream
2 teaspoons thyme, chopped
Seasoning

Chop the butter into the flour and either rub the fat into the
flour by hand, or whiz in a food processor, with a pinch of salt.
Break up the egg yolks slightly with a fork and gradually add
them, and if necessary a little chilled water, to the flour
mixture until it coheres into a ball. Wrap this and chill it in the
fridge for 30 minutes. Set the oven to heat at 190°C, 375°F,
Gas 5.

Meanwhile, skin the tomatoes by cutting a cross in the skin at
the base and dropping them one or two at a time into boiling
water for about 30 seconds. Cool them briefly in cold water so
that you can handle them, and then, working from the cross cut,
pull the skin away. Slice them and put them into a sieve over a
bowl to drain.

Roll out the pastry into a large round and place on an oven-
proof pizza plate or baking tray. Prick the pastry with a fork
and give it 10 minutes or so in the oven until coloured. With a
fork, break up the egg white and use it to paint the pastry all
over. Put the pastry back in the oven for a further 5 minutes.

Spread the tomato slices on the pastry and sprinkle them with
the cream, seasoning and the thyme. Give it 10-15 minutes in
the oven to heat through thoroughly. Serves 4-6 as a starter.

FENNEL WITH THYME

    2 large fennel bulbs, quartered, cores trimmed
    3-4 tablespoons olive oil
    2-3 teaspoons thyme leaves
    100ml white wine
    Salt and pepper

Preheat the oven to 180°C, 350°F, Gas 4. Heat the oil in a
frying pan and sauté the fennel until it is well coloured.
Transfer it to a small roasting pan and sprinkle the wine over
it. Scatter the thyme over the fennel with some salt and pepper
and any remaining oil. Cook in the oven for 45-60 minutes,
turning the fennel once or twice while cooking. Serves 4.

ROAST PARSNIPS WITH HONEY AND THYME

This recipe comes from Jenny Leggatt's *Cooking with Flowers*.

450g parsnips
1-2 tablespoons clear honey
1 tablespoon oil
2 tablespoons thyme
Salt and pepper

Heat the oven to 190°C, 375°F, Gas 5. Mix the honey and oil together and coat the parsnips in the mixture. Place the parsnips in a baking dish and sprinkle with salt and pepper and then with the thyme. Bake for about 1 hour, basting from time to time. Serve sprinkled with fresh thyme - include some of the flowers if you have them. Serves 4.

WATERCRESS
Rorippa nasturtium-aquaticum

WATERCRESS SOUP

150g watercress
1 onion, finely chopped
250g potatoes, peeled and diced
900ml stock
100ml single cream
Salt and pepper

Soften the onion for 2-3 minutes in the oil in a pan with the lid on. Add the potato, watercress stems and stock and simmer for 30 minutes until the potato is cooked. Put some of the best leaves on one side but add the rest to the soup and cook for 5 minutes. Allow to cool a little and then purée in a liquidiser or food processor. Return to the pan, stir in the cream and season to taste. Reheat briefly if necessary before serving, but do not boil. Stir in the reserved watercress, finely chopped, at the last moment. Serves 4.

GREEN VEGETABLE RISOTTO
This recipe is from *Is there a Nutmeg in the House?*, a posthumous anthology of work by Elizabeth David.

300-350g arborio rice
2 shallots, chopped
3 courgettes, diced
1 bunch watercress
100g butter
1¼ litres hot water
3 tablespoons grated Parmesan cheese
Nutmeg and salt

Using a small pan, cook the courgettes in 30g of the butter until just soft. Set aside. Wash the watercress and discard any stems sprouting roots. Put another 15g butter in your pan and cook the watercress for 1 minute. Turn it out onto a plate and chop it with a knife. Then take a large heavy pan and soften the shallots without browning in a further 45g of the butter. Add the rice and stir round until it is all shiny with the butter. Stir in 600ml of boiling water and some salt. Cook over a moderate heat without a lid until all the liquid is absorbed, which will take perhaps 15 minutes. Keep an eye on it and if it seems to be getting too dry add some more hot water. The rice should be just resistant to the teeth and the consistency of the risotto should be liquid. When the rice is ready add the courgettes and the watercress, stirring with a wooden fork. Finally add the Parmesan, the remaining butter and a little grated nutmeg. Serve in bowls with extra Parmesan on the table. Serves 4.

WATERCRESS MAYONNAISE

2 large egg yolks
½ level teaspoon salt
½ level teaspoon dry mustard
Pinch of caster sugar
300ml olive or other oil, according to taste
50ml wine vinegar
½ bunch of watercress

First ensure that the ingredients are at room temperature. Put the yolks into a bowl with the salt, mustard, sugar and 2 teaspoons of the vinegar. Beat well, using a wooden spoon or whisk. Start to add the oil, drop by drop, beating all the time until the mixture stiffens. Thin again with 2 teaspoons of vinegar and, still beating, slowly add the rest of the oil in a continuous stream. Stir in the remaining vinegar and adjust the seasoning if you think it needs it. Lastly stir in ½-1 tablespoon of boiling water.

Pick over the watercress and discard any thick stems or sprouting parts. Chop the remainder finely and stir into the mayonnaise. This is lovely with cold fish, or you could use it in the next recipe. Serves 6.

EGGS WITH WATERCRESS
This recipe comes from *The Best of Cordon Bleu* by Rosemary Hume and Muriel Downes.

6 very fresh small eggs
2 bunches watercress
300ml thick mayonnaise
2-3 tablespoons vinaigrette dressing
A dash of Tabasco sauce
A little lemon juice

Poach the eggs neatly and when firm lift them out and slide carefully into a bowl of cold water. Bring some slightly salted water to the boil in a pan and add to it half a bunch of watercress. Simmer for a few minutes until soft and then drain the watercress thoroughly and press it through a sieve to produce 1-2 teaspoons of purée. Break the rest of the watercress into small sprigs, discarding the coarsest stems and arrange on six plates. Moisten with the vinaigrette mixed with the Tabasco. Lift the eggs from the water and dry them well on paper towels. Place one egg on each portion of watercress. Stir the purée and lemon juice to taste into the mayonnaise (if using commercial mayonnaise you may wish to thin it with some plain yoghurt) and spoon some over each dish. Serve with some wholemeal bread and butter. Serves 6 as a starter.

WATERCRESS AND ALMOND PESTO

This recipe was given by Sue Lawrence in her column in *Scotland on Sunday*.

100g watercress, washed
3 tablespoons freshly grated Parmesan cheese
50g whole almonds in their skins
1 clove garlic, peeled and chopped
6-7 tablespoons good olive oil
Sea salt

Place the first four ingredients in a food processor and whiz briefly. Slowly add oil to combine everything into a thick paste. You may not need all the oil. Add salt to taste. This pesto is great stirred into pasta or with white fish.

PORK WITH WATERCRESS AND TOMATO

This recipe is given by kind permission of Sainsbury's Supermarkets Ltd.

500g pork tenderloin
2 tablespoons oil from sundried tomatoes
3 tablespoons Worcestershire sauce
2 cloves garlic
250ml natural Greek yoghurt
2 tablespoons sundried tomato paste
50g watercress, finely chopped
½ small onion, finely chopped
50g sundried tomatoes, drained and chopped
Salt and ground black pepper

Cut the pork into slices approximately 2cm thick and place them in a dish with the tomato oil, Worcestershire sauce and garlic. Stir it all round and leave to marinate for at least 20 minutes. Mix together the yoghurt, tomato paste, watercress, onion, chopped tomatoes and seasoning to taste. Put aside to chill until required. When you are ready to cook the pork, heat some of the marinade in a frying pan over a moderate heat. Add the pork and cook it for 8-10 minutes, turning it and keeping it moving. Serve it with rice or pasta, garnished with watercress sprigs, and hand the sauce separately. Serves 4.

WILD DUCK
Anas platyrhynchos, crecca

These recipes will work quite well with farmed duck, allowing for the probably greater size.

WILD DUCK WITH CIDER AND APPLES
Claire Macdonald (www.claire-macdonald.com) gives this tasty recipe in *More Seasonal Cooking*.

  2 mallard or other ducks, approximately 1kg each
  2 small onions, skinned and left whole
  1 apple, cut in half
  75g butter
  1 tablespoon oil
  2 medium onions, skinned and sliced
  750g apples, eating and cooking varieties mixed
  Salt and ground black pepper
  600ml dry cider
  150ml double cream

Put 1 small onion and half an apple into the cavity of each duck. Heat the butter and oil together in a heavy pan and brown the ducks well all over. Take the birds out and keep warm. Now add the sliced onions to the pan, and cook gently for about 5 minutes without browning. Peel, core and slice the mixed apples and add to the onions in the pan. Season with salt and pepper and pour on the cider. Return the ducks to the pan, cover with a tight-fitting lid and simmer very gently for 1 hour. Test that the ducks are cooked by checking that the juices show no trace of pink when the thick part of the meat is pierced with a sharp knife. Remove the ducks from the pan and stir in the cream and adjust the seasoning to make the sauce. To serve, carve the ducks and spoon the sauce over the slices. Serves 4-6.

BRAISED MALLARD AND CHERRIES
This recipe comes from *Game Cooking* by Lilli Gore.

> 2 mallards
> 1 lemon, cut in two
> Salt and pepper
> 2 small potatoes, peeled
> 2 onions, skinned
> 80g butter
> 1 tablespoon flour
> 1 glass sherry
> 250g stoned black cherries (fresh or tinned)
> Stock

Dip the lemon halves into a mixture of pepper and salt, and then use them to rub the ducks inside and out. Put an onion and a potato inside each bird. In a frying pan brown the birds in the butter, and then transfer them to a heavy casserole. Add the cherries. Stir the flour into the remaining fat in the frying pan and over gentle heat add the sherry gradually. You will need some of the juice from the cherries, or some stock if using fresh fruit, to make a thick pouring sauce. Pour it over the ducks in the casserole, cover tightly and simmer for 1 hour until the ducks are tender. Check at half time and add a little more stock if necessary. Serves 4-6 depending on the size of the birds.

SALAD OF WILD DUCK

> Cold roast duck, cut in slivers
> 1 persimmon (Sharon fruit), halved and sliced
> 1 avocado, halved, peeled and sliced
> Vinaigrette dressing

Arrange the duck and fruit on a bed of green leaves. Spoon over the dressing and scatter with chopped parsley. Serves 2.

CUMBERLAND SAUCE - to serve with cold roast wild duck.

150ml red wine or ruby port
250 g redcurrant jelly
1 Seville orange
1 lemon
1 small onion, finely chopped
1 tablespoon caster sugar
1 level teaspoon dry mustard
2 cloves
Salt and pepper

Grate or cut into fine strips the orange and lemon rind and blanch in boiling water. Set aside. Squeeze the juice from the fruit and put it in a pan with all the other ingredients. Bring slowly to the boil stirring all the time. Lower the heat and simmer gently with the lid on for 15 minutes. Add the orange and lemon rind and continue to simmer for another 5 minutes. Allow to cool, fish out the cloves, and without straining it, serve the sauce poured over the cold meat.

ACKNOWLEDGEMENTS

When I embarked on this project three years ago I had no idea of just how much it would entail. I am deeply grateful therefore to all who have offered me assistance along the way.

In particular I should like to mention Robin and K Orr who gave advice on presentation, Nichola Fletcher, Clarissa Dickson Wright and Sue Lawrence who advised on copyright issues, Annie Rhodes without whom the book might never have appeared, and not least, Claudia Pottier on whose horticultural skills the whole edifice is dependent. Katherine Mercer and Roger Mercer read the late stages of the text and saved me from sundry errors and infelicities; Andrew Mercer was invaluable whenever I failed to control the computer. To all these people I tender thanks.

In addition I am grateful to all friends who took an interest, who gave encouragement and recipes, who made garden produce available to me, and who cheerfully tasted as I cooked and cooked again the many candidates for inclusion in this book.

"Eggs Cooked with Marigold" and "Orange Mint Salad" from *The Gentle Art of Cookery* by Mrs C. F. Leyel and Miss Olga Hartley, published by The Hogarth Press, are reprinted by permission of The Random House Group Ltd, and I heartily thank all the cooks, cookery writers and publishers who have given me permission to use their recipes.

Every effort has been made to contact all copyright holders but in a few instances, unfortunately, this has not proved possible. Writers and sources have been given throughout.

SJM

INDEX

INDEX